Training in Motion

Training in Motion

HOW TO USE MOVEMENT
TO CREATE ENGAGING
AND EFFECTIVE LEARNING

Mike Kuczala

AMACOM

American Management Association
New York · Atlanta · Brussels · Chicago · Mexico City · San Francisco
Shanghai · Tokyo · Toronto · Washington, D. C.

Bulk discounts available. For details visit:
www.amacombooks.org/go/specialsales
Or contact special sales:
Phone: 800-250-5308
Email: specialsls@amanet.org
View all the AMACOM titles at: www.amacombooks.org
American Management Association: www.amanet.org

This publication is designed to provide accurate and authoritative information in regard to the subject matter covered. It is sold with the understanding that the publisher is not engaged in rendering legal, accounting, or other professional service. If legal advice or other expert assistance is required, the services of a competent professional person should be sought.

Library of Congress Cataloging-in-Publication Data

Kuczala, Mike.
    Training in motion : how to use movement to create engaging and effective learning / Mike Kuczala. — First Edition.
        pages cm
    Includes bibliographical references and index.
    ISBN 978-0-8144-3494-9 (pbk.) — ISBN 0-8144-3494-0 (pbk.) — ISBN 978-0-8144-3495-6 (ebook)
1. Movement, Psychology of. 2. Brain stimulation. 3. Movement education. I. Title.
    BF295.K83 2015
    153.1′53—dc23   2015010238

About AMA
American Management Association (www.amanet.org) is a world leader in talent development, advancing the skills of individuals to drive business success. Our mission is to support the goals of individuals and organizations through a complete range of products and services, including classroom and virtual seminars, webcasts, webinars, podcasts, conferences, corporate and government solutions, business books, and research. AMA's approach to improving performance combines experiential learning—learning through doing—with opportunities for ongoing professional growth at every step of one's career journey.

Printing number

10 9 8 7 6 5 4 3 2 1

This book is dedicated to the many students, both adults and children, that I have had the pleasure of knowing over the past three decades. I learned far more from you than I could have ever imparted. Thank you.

Contents

APPENDIXES

Foreword

Several years ago, I was conducting a "train-the-trainer" program, and I asked people what they wanted out of the course. Most of the answers were traditional responses, but one surprised me. The individual, who had been in one of my programs before, sat up and said, "I want to train and educate people like you do. You not only make it fun and engaging, but people remember and apply what they have learned in a way that I have never experienced before. I am back to learn what you do and how you do it." I was humbled, but not at my abilities. Rather, I understood that I had learned my techniques from Mike Kuczala.

The purpose of *Training in Motion* is to do something that the traditional texts do not teach, and that is to make your training more effective by tailoring your delivery and content to the way the brain and body learn best. Movement matters, and *Training in Motion* is practical, realistic, and simple to use. It will give you results. After reading this book and incorporating Mike's principles into your teaching, an average trainer will become good, and the good trainer will become great.

As a human resources executive, professional trainer, and academic, the material contained in *Training in Motion* is relevant to most aspects of my work. First, the book is written in a manner that is easy to understand, easy to explain, and easy to implement. It is logical. The activities contained in each chapter actually put into practice what you have read and learned. In addition, as a training and learning professional, it helps you to understand the reason behind what you are doing, why it works, how to do it, and things to avoid. This book gives you the tools to you need. *Training in Motion* is not about games trainers play. For those of us who train professionally, training is not a game. Rather it is about the principles, practices, activities, and exercises that enhance the transfer of knowledge, skills, and abilities. *Training in Motion* makes learning come alive.

When I was asked to write the Foreword to Mike's book, I was floored. My first reaction was, couldn't they get anyone else? But Mike told me he didn't want anyone else. I thought about our first meeting. It was several weeks after I experienced Mike's program that focused on classroom learning for children. His first book, *The Kinesthetic Classroom,* is a fantastic tool for those in that line of work. It changed the way I taught younger people. As a corporate person, I knew applying those elements would rock the training world. After the session, we briefly talked about how the same concepts could be applied to training in the business world. As a follow up, we had dinner at a Korean restaurant in Manhattan. We talked about how to use Mike's expertise in a way that is currently not being done on a large scale in corporations. There are a lot of trainers peddling their services, but not a lot of great trainers. We talked about writing a book. I forgot about that until Mike asked me to write this Foreword. Successful people say what they will do and do what they say they will do. I expect that *Training in Motion* will allow you to reach a new level of effectiveness and professional development as it did for me.

Josh Friedlander
Chief Human Resources Officer
Latham & Watkins

Preface

Our innate desire to be in constant motion is a key survival characteristic of humans. People pace when forced to stand in a line or doodle on a piece of paper if caught in a boring meeting. Certainly, technological gadgetry and the expectation that we need to be in constant contact with the world is partly to blame, but at the heart of all this caged up "gotta move" behavior is a basic, instinctual need for movement.

The activities and exercises offered in this book are all grounded in this instinctual need to involve our bodies in the learning experience. Solid research and my experience as a learning professional back this kinetic connection, as well as support the assertion in this book that introducing movement into learning experiences creates more positive training and workplace environments that are underscored by optimism, trust, enthusiasm, joy, and passion to perform at a higher level.

The magic of movement is very real. My work with thousands of leaders, salespeople, teachers, administrators, coaches, organizations, athletes, musicians, and others have convinced me of its capability in both educational and corporate settings.

Moreover, this experience has convinced me that instructional designers, facilitators, and traditional classroom trainers who don't take full advantage of the transformative power of movement are leaving a powerful learning tool on the table to the detriment of their learners and the organizations that employ them.

For the learners, static training events—seated, listening, taking notes, very little interaction if any at all—are less enjoyable and lack the important element of human connection with other participants. For the organizations, the loss is more profound and ultimately more dangerous. It means training participants who are significantly less able to apply what they've learned back on the job based on what is known about how the brain engages the world and how the brain prefers to learn.

And that's a bottom-line performance price no organization can afford to pay. It is my hope that this book builds a critical awareness among all practicing learning professionals, including coaches, mentors, trainers, facilitators, and instructional designers.

Acknowledgments

I would like to give special thanks to the following people:

- Josh Friedlander for putting this vision in motion.
- Chris Heinly for your trust, friendship, and a place to get started.
- Pat Shields for your continued belief, support, and friendship.
- Traci Lengel for your brilliance and inspiration.
- Mark Morrow for your guidance and expertise throughout this project.
- William Helms for your guidance, expertise, professionalism, vision, and patience.

The Connection That Moves You

- Chapter 1—Connecting Movement to a Learning Brain
- Chapter 2—Training with the Brain in Mind
- Chapter 3—Applying the Benefits of Movement

These three chapters provide a basic grounding in brain research that demonstrates how these findings are incorporated into training and other learning events. The section also explains eight specific benefits that come from using movement to enhance both the learner experience and expected organizational results.

Chapter 1 sets the stage with an exploration of the key theories, conclusions, and assumptions about the power of movement to increase the effectiveness of learning events.

Chapter 2 demonstrates how these practices have been validated and, in some cases, challenged by brain science conducted over the last twenty years.

Chapter 3 further deconstructs these recent findings to offer eight ways that movement enhances learning outcomes, along with other key recommended learning strategies.

CHAPTER 1

Connecting Movement to a Learning Brain

Despite the development of sophisticated distance learning technologies that allow learners to access training from any place or at any time using the most convenient device they have on hand (a desktop computer, tablet, laptop, or smartphone), a majority of training still occurs in traditional classroom settings.

Such a statistic is hardly a surprise to trainers who increasingly use these advanced learning tools but still find they spend a considerable amount of time in physical classrooms. One reason that classroom training remains the predominant delivery method is that eLearning is not appropriate for all types of training, as, for example, when role play is essential to the training. A more important reason, a least from my perspective, is that the connection and collaboration between learners in a classroom fulfills our human need for community, and it is this connection that fosters greater learning success.

The learning techniques described in this book are likely familiar to experienced learning professionals. What this book shows is a direct connection between movement and well understood and researched conclusions based on brain research. More importantly, it shows readers how to tap into this valuable learning wellspring and make movement a reliable training effectiveness ally.

MAKING A CONNECTION

I am not neuroscientist or a doctor. I'm not even a researcher. I am just someone who has spent years reading everything I could get my hands on about how the human brain learns, and in particular, how to take advantage of the intrinsic connection between movement and learning. This intense passion has been at the center of my professional work for the last 20 years and it underscores every written or training/learning contribution I've made to the field, including this book.

The roots of this book reach back to 2006, when I collaborated with Traci Lengel, a dynamic and successful Health and Physical Educator in northern Pennsylvania, to create a graduate course called *It's All About You: Wellness and School*. The course, offered by the Regional Training Center to Pennsylvania, Maryland, and New Jersey, included my previous nutrition training work along with significant portions of my work discussed in this book—the brain/body connection, physical fitness, stress management, time management, and social wellness.

As it turned out, the course was very popular with its target audience—educators—who used the positive life-changing information they discovered through the class to change the learning dynamics in their own classes. Based on the success of this class, Traci and I decided to collaborate on a second training design that focused on the connection between movement and learning.

In 2008, we field tested a course called *The Kinesthetic Classroom: Teaching and Learning Through Movement*. This course was also a success and, in fact, it became one of the most successful courses in the

25-year history of the Regional Training Center. The course included a Six-Part Framework for using movement that Traci created and I helped her fine tune. The framework makes movement user friendly and accessible to all teachers in all content areas and at all grade levels. Dozens of instructors now teach this course to thousands of teachers in Pennsylvania, New Jersey, and Maryland, who use the concepts to improve learning outcomes in their classes.

Another positive outcome of my work with Traci was the publication in 2010 of our bestselling book, *The Kinesthetic Classroom: Teaching and Learning Through Movement*. *Training in Motion* goes beyond *The Kinesthetic Classroom* to include information about connecting cognitive function, physical fitness, and movement theories to both effective teaching and improved facilitation abilities.

As a full-fledged brain and movement enthusiast, I want *Training in Motion* to inform corporate trainers and other learning professionals about taking advantage of this brain/body connection to improve the effectiveness and bottom-line value of their training and learning programs.

BRAIN BASICS

Training in Motion is a book about using movement to enhance the training process so I will reference—directly or indirectly—the conclusions or implications of brain research throughout. However, the reason for this introduction on brain basics is to provide grounding and context for the discussion that follows and a baseline brain-related vocabulary to guide your learning.

So, to begin with, here are some interesting facts about the brain according to Sousa (2011). The brain:

- Weighs a little more than three pounds.
- Is about the size of a small grapefruit.

- Is shaped like a walnut.
- Represents about 2 percent of our body weight but burns almost 20 percent of our calories.
- Contains approximately a trillion cells made up of neurons (specialized cells that process information) and glial cells that support and protect the neurons. Neural connections and networks are at the core of learning and memory.

Some Parts of the Brain

To understand the brain, it's helpful to divide it into **exterior parts (lobes) and interior parts**. Each has unique qualities, traits, and specialties.

First, the exterior parts: Have you ever forgotten something important and **hit yourself in the forehead with the palm of your hand**? If you have, you've directly connected with your brain's **frontal lobe,** which is one of the four major areas (lobes) of the exterior human brain. This area is the executive control center and personality area; its job is planning and thinking (for example, making plans for a 2:00 dental appointment and then forgetting to show up). This is the area of the brain that also curbs emotional excess and helps us solve problems.

Every time you wash your hair and massage the area above your ears you're making a connection with your brain's **temporal lobes,** which are responsible for processing sound and language.

If you've ever sat back in your desk chair and clasped your hands behind your head to stretch or relax and enjoy a moment of satisfaction or deep thought, your hands are embracing the brain's **occipital lobes,** which are responsible for visual processing. And, if you happen to be in the habit of clasping your hands near the top of your head, you're showing some love for your brain's **parietal lobe,** which is responsible for processing sensory information, spatial orientation, and calculations.

Finally, if you comb your hair from the middle of your head (more common among women these days, but it was a men's style in the 1970s), then you are raking your comb across the area of your brain at the very top called the **somatosensory cortex** (directly in front of the parietal lobe), which is responsible for processing touch signals. Combing your hair this way also connects you with your brain's **motor cortex (directly in back of the frontal lobe)**, which is responsible for coordinating body movement (see Figure 1.1).

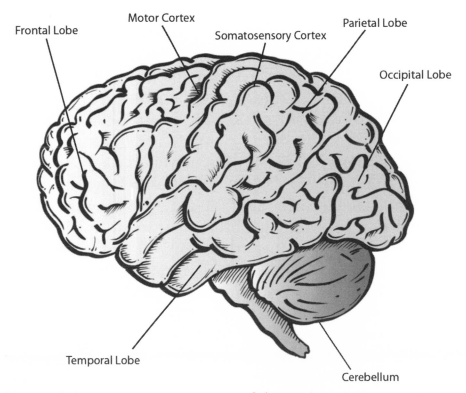

Figure 1.1 Some Exterior Parts of the Brain

Clearly, the brain is a much more complicated organ than this simple tour, but our description serves two purposes. First, it's a very graphic way of explaining the concepts, and second, if you pretend to make the movements suggested—hitting your forehead, washing and combing your hair—then you are validating the underlying premise of this book of connecting movement to learning.

Interior Parts of the Brain

Physically touching the **interior parts** of your brain as an aid to learning is obviously not possible, so I'll use a two-story house with a basement as a learning analogy. First, think of the **brain stem** as your brain's basement. Nearly all homes locate basic infrastructure and operational connections in the basement, such as plumbing, electrical, cable, telephone connections, and heating and air conditioning equipment. Our brain's basic survival connections and functionality, including the regulation of our heartbeat, respiration, body temperature, and digestion, are all centered in the brain's basement.

Most of the life of a typical home happens in the kitchen, living or family, and dining rooms. The brain's **limbic system,** located above the brain stem basement and below the cerebrum (a typical home's second floor) is composed of four principal "living" areas that are called the **thalamus, hypothalamus, hippocampus, and amygdala**. Though the limbic system is not limited to these four structures, these areas are the most important for this book because they relate to learning and memory.

The **thalamus** processes all sensory information, except for smell. The **hypothalamus** maintains homeostasis and monitors things such as sleep and the intake of food and liquid. Of the four, the **hippocampus** and **amygdala** are more relevant to the training and learning process since one of the major roles of the hippocampus is to convert information in working memory (or temporary short-term memory) to long-term storage—very important to a trainer.

When information enters working memory, the hippocampus essentially searches long-term memory files and compares it to the new information. It is this comparison process for both relevancy and meaning that is most important for trainers, because making this connection is key to the long-term storage and recall of information.

The amygdala processes and encodes emotion. Take a moment to think about your most potent memory and the emotion attached to it. You're more likely to remember every detail about the day you fell in love, but have less emotional memories about the day you memorized the names of all the continents of the world. It is this amygdala emotional encoding that makes the difference.

The attic of your brain is the **cerebrum.** Note that the analogy breaks down a bit here since your brain's attic carries nearly 80 percent of the house by weight and is separated into two nearly identical haves connected by a thick bundle of electrical fibers running down the center. Still, the brain's attic remains a place for deep thought and concentration.

The control center for all movement in the house, called the cerebellum, is at the rear and is just below the attic. The cerebellum coordinates movement and plays a critical role in the performance of motor tasks. It works with the motor cortex to coordinate the learning of motor skills (see Figure 1.2).

Finally, connecting the wireless lifeblood of our physical home these days are our wireless modems that connect all our essential devices—computers, smartphones, Netflix viewing.

In this house analogy, consider the nearly 100 billion neurons that provide both the energy and connection vital for living. The

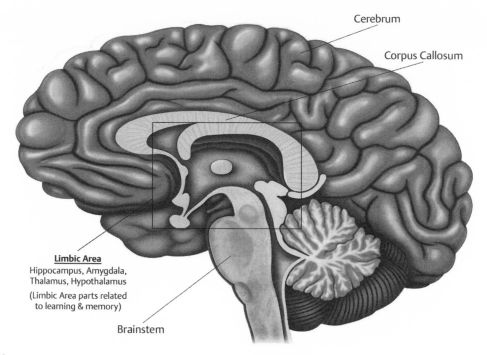

Figure 1.2 Some Exterior Parts of the Brain

special difference between a physical home's wireless systems and the brain's neurons is that neurons have the ability to grow and make new connections with each other through chemical messengers called neurotransmitters (dopamine, serotonin, etc.) that leads to learning. And, when strong networks are formed, information from these neural communities is more easily retrieved.

KEY CONCEPTS

- Movement can play a powerful role in learning, training, and training design.
- The discussed exterior parts of the brain include the frontal lobe, parietal lobe, temporal lobe, occipital lobe, motor cortex, and somatosensory cortex.

■ The discussed interior parts of the brain include the cerebrum, cerebellum, amygdala, thalamus, hypothalamus, hippocampus, and brain stem.

■ Neurons create the complex networks that form memories and learning.

■ Emotion is a powerful player in learning and memory that impacts learning both negatively and positively.

CHAPTER 2

Training with the Brain in Mind

WHY MOVEMENT CREATES ENGAGEMENT

Trust me, I am no scientist, but the topic of brain research has fascinated me for years, especially brain research related to how humans acquire and process new information. In fact, over the last thirty years, research focusing on the specific neural pathways used for learning has fundamentally altered many of our assumptions about the optimal conditions for learning.

> *The human brain has 100 billion neurons, each neuron connected to ten thousand other neurons. Sitting on your shoulders is the most complicated object in the known universe.*
> Michiko Kaku, author, futurist, and theoretical physicist

While it would be easy to cite dozens of important, critical findings from this extensive body of research, an important synthesis of brain research as it applies to learning was created by educator

Lee Oberparleiter. Through both an examination of an expansive body of literature on brain research, and 35 years of public, private, and higher education instruction, Oberparleiter developed what he calls the 12 brain-compatible principles. Movement can play a direct role in eight of those principles during a training experience. You might think of these eight principles as nonnegotiable brain facts that must be factored into every learning event to ensure a return on your training investment.[1]

Unfortunately, these simple principles are not used more consistently, mostly because neuroscience is a relatively new field and the information is simply not widely shared among teachers, trainers, and other learning professionals. And, even if this information were widely distributed, it's just human nature to lean on what we know, the tried-and-true methods and models that we're comfortable using (mostly lecture and PowerPoint slides) as opposed to other methods that are still fairly new. That's unfortunate, because learners are not getting the full benefit from their training and training professionals are missing the opportunity to demonstrate the value and potential of training to increase productivity and provide return on investment to their organizations.

EIGHT BRAIN PRINCIPLES YOU NEED TO KNOW

The eight brain principles that follow are supported by research conducted over the past three decades. If you're interested in some of the supporting research, see the references at the back of this book. For now, just focus on applying these discoveries about how our brains acquire and store information so you will become a more effective and valuable learning professional.

1. **Our brain is preprogramed to notice novelty in the surrounding environment.** Our brain is preprogrammed (as

part of our brain's survival mode wiring) to notice changes and differences in the environment. At some point, learners will zone out as they search for this environmental variety. Participants begin scanning their surroundings for something more interesting to focus on and, as a result, one PowerPoint slide begins to look like the one before it. Once our brains switch to this survival mode tactic, anything not engaging, relevant, or meaningful to the task at hand (survival) is dismissed. That's why learners respond so well to novelty in their environment. Changing up the environment resets this innate scanning switch and allows for focused attention from your learners.

2. **Learning and movement are innately connected in the human brain.** Learning and movement are closely related. Just as the brain scans its surroundings for changes that indicate potential threats, our brain is preprogrammed to learn directly through the movement of our own body and through observation of other humans in motion. That's why learning new concepts and taking in new information through the use of our bodies is one of the most effective learning technologies available to trainers. It's all about implicit learning (learning by doing, feeling, or seeing, often on a subconscious level)—the brain's preferred way to learn. Demonstration can also be an effective and related learning tool. We observe the movements required to produce a result or accomplish a task and then simply mimic what we see. Despite the fact that most of us are efficient visual or kinesthetic learners, long-established learning conventions usually force us to learn through what we read and hear, that is, through traditional training methods.

3. **Learning is enhanced when we connect and communicate with others.** Early in the process of evolution humans learned

that group safety, comfort, and productivity is ensured by banding together in groups. In other words, humans are naturally drawn toward cooperation and collective learning. By managing this basic need for connection and community in your classroom, you'll increase the likelihood that more of the information you present will be stored in long-term memory and retained for later use.

4. **Emotional connection enhances the learning experience.** We all know our most memorable experiences are directly linked to our emotional responses to these unique circumstances or life milestones. Anything we experience on a truly emotional level is etched permanently in our memory. Nostalgia can play a powerful role in establishing these emotional connections, as we often experience the same emotions that we had experienced during an event that occurred even decades ago when we reflect back in time. Advertisers and marketers use this powerful craving for emotional connection through period specific music or by displaying images that celebrate nationality, family and home life, and, yes, puppies. Learning programs and events that miss this opportunity for learners to connect emotionally are ignoring a powerful learning retention tool. The amygdala located in the center of the brain checks all incoming sensory data for emotional content and is responsible for processing emotion. If a strong enough emotion is detected, the amygdala will boost neurotransmitters responsible for long-term memory storage. That's not to say that all emotional experiences and any connected learning will always be stored permanently, but it does demonstrate the power of emotion in our lives and why this innate part of our brain's functioning should definitely be in your training effectiveness tool kit.

5. **Learn by doing is a fundamental learning preference.** Here's another concept we all accept as true from experience, yet many training events don't include any actual hands-on activities and experiences. Imagine how many words it would take to explain each step of changing a car tire. Without question, the document would be lengthy, confusing, and most likely not produce the intended result. Demonstration, on the other hand, requires few words, and the learner can become an expert after practicing the technique a few times. The lesson is clear; the most effective training is hands on, concrete, and directly applicable to what actions are required to produce the desirable outcome. Would you fly with a pilot who had only been lectured on how to fly or choose a surgeon based on PowerPoint training slides? They key phrase is "learn by doing." In both cases, the long hours of study and demonstration are only as effective as the follow-up practice that occurs. The risk of losing or forgetting information rises dramatically when the correct technique is not practiced enough to be able to perform the task well.

6. **Connecting new knowledge to old knowledge improves retention.** Have you ever wondered why the proverbial "lightbulb" lights up in our heads when we connect new information to something we already know? Simply put, our brains are wired to make this connection and, even better, making this connection makes us feel good. When confronted with new data, the hippocampus instantly checks long-term storage for relevancy. It does this implicitly (subconsciously). If the hippocampus can't determine a connection, or relevancy, the new information is likely to be lost unless the learner is given more time to practice and rehearse the new information. Without this connection, our brains are forced to work

a lot harder, as they try to sort out the relevancy of new information. It's great to learn new concepts and challenge our brains to work hard, but when you are charged with ensuring productivity-boosting retention, nothing beats relevancy.

7. **Downtime is required to ensure new learning is processed and stored.** In general, anything you still remember the next day has a very good chance of making it to permanent memory (although there is always a chance of forgetting). That's because sleep (actually the Rapid Eye Movement [REM] phases) serves as the brain's "off-line" switch, and this down time allows the hippocampus to encode new information into permanent memory. A "typical" eight-to-nine-hour night of sleep provides five REM cycles. The lesson for trainers is twofold.

    i.   Transferring new information to long-term memory is supported by repetition and time away from learning activities. Short bursts of content followed by review, practice, and rehearsal provide the opportunity for information to be transferred to the permanent memory lock box. In general, learning activities should not exceed the working memory capacity of an adult—about three-to-five chunks of unrelated information at one time.[2]

    ii. Participants might feel confident about what they've learned after a first day of training, but any assumed retention should be checked the next day to make sure sleep has done its job of firmly cementing the content in long-term memory.

8. **Stress seriously impacts our ability to learn.** Which one of these trainers would have the most success with a room full of learners? A trainer who waves a gun and screams to make important points; a trainer who uses inappropriate and up-

setting examples to illustrate learning points; or a trainer who begins each class with calm, relaxing music and a meditation exercise.

Certainly, the stressed and emotionally charged sessions will garner our attention since our brains naturally give priority to anything in the environment that threatens survival or is emotionally charged.[3] But excessive stress is detrimental to learning and it creates an information roadblock. On the other hand, a calm brain is a learning brain so the ideal trainer is the one who uses stress releasing activities that increase the participant's learning capacity. Here's why:

Our brain prioritizes data it receives on three levels: (1) data that impacts survival; (2) data that creates an emotional response and; (3) new data it needs to process.[4] Survival and emotional responses to information naturally create stress, but this is not the optimal environment for learning. A low-stress, highly engaging environment works best to encourage learning.

LONG-TERM MEMORY

Another key memory mechanism to understand is described in Marilee Sprenger's 1999 book, *Learning and Memory: The Brain in Action.* Essentially, Sprenger's book revealed five different memory pathways our brain uses to store information in long-term memory.[7]

1. **Semantic.** This pathway deals with facts and figures that may or may not be related to a specific learning and is described as information we "know." For example, you know that George Washington was the first President of the United States; that 24 divided by 8 is 3; and that Los Angeles is in California.

2. **Episodic.** This is associated with a mental picture of the location where an event or learning occurred. For example, remembering the details of the building where you were married or of the college classroom where you learned about macroeconomics. This lane handles memories about events in our life. Our brains create specific "learning addresses" that describe where information was first learned. As a trainer, you can use this to your advantage by asking participants to change where they sit when the content focus changes.

3. **Emotional.** Emotional memory is the most potent of all lanes and is where events are stored quickly and permanently. You can try this pathway out right now by taking a moment to think about some of your most potent and emotional memories. It's unlikely that any of your memories involve sitting in a required class that doesn't hold any interest for you.

4. **Automatic Memory.** This pathway is for information that is automatically accessed and readily available. Any learning that has become automatic, such as certain mathematical functions or decoding abilities is most likely stored in this lane.

5. **Procedural.** This includes the learning of a physical skill acquired through practice and experience, such as riding a bike, playing a musical instrument, swinging a baseball bat, or kicking a soccer ball. Procedural learning refers to skills that have become routine.

It's important to understand that these pathways operate either independently or together to support learning outcomes. New brain research shows that automatic and procedural learning, traditionally connected to movement functions in the brain's cerebellum are also connected to the other three memory lanes and support emotions, memory, cognition, analysis, and decision making.[8,9]

THE LIMITS OF MEMORY

Learning professionals need a working knowledge of how the brain processes and stores information. Without this knowledge, even the most inspirational trainer or facilitator won't be able to engage audiences in ways that encourage information recall. Here are some big-picture memory basics to consider.

In a most basic interpretation, our brains process information on two levels. The top level is designed to hold data temporarily while it is being processed and readied for permanent storage in long-term memory. In a computer, this temporary holding area is called random access memory (RAM). In the human brain, this processing function is simply called short-term memory (now divided into immediate and working memory). The one difference between a computer's RAM and our short-term memory is that our brain does impose time and capacity parameters.[5] We can only hold on to so much information at one time. However, processing is a key to the ability of both humans and computers to process and prepare data—which could take days or months. Without the luxury of time and rehearsal, a crash of sorts occurs and the data is lost.

SIX LONG-TERM MEMORY TECHNIQUES

In practical terms, this means that nearly all new information will be forgotten unless it's associated with some engaging, emotional, or interesting experience. Most learning professionals know by experience that this connection is important, but here are six simple but effective techniques you can use to help learners connect with your training content.[6]

1. Create memorable patterns that allow learners to predict future questions, events, or problems, so that these answers are

more easily derived by participants. It is critical to take great care not to create material that bores participants or undervalues their intelligence.

2. Connect new content to familiar concepts or those based on prior knowledge. For example, new software training that is built around similarities and differences builds cognitive bridges for your participants.

3. Encourage a personal interest investment in the training content. For example, you might have participants create personal learning goals and then compare them with the learning objectives set out for the class to build a case for content relevancy and interest.

4. Associate new content with prior experiences. For example, if you were training new leaders to listen effectively, you might ask participants to consider or discuss how they felt when someone dismissed their ideas or their own difficulties listening to others.

5. Support emotional engagement. Everyone likes to hear a good story, so when possible introduce a compelling narrative. For example, I often use a personal story about how I became a music major and eventually earned both a bachelor's and master's degree without ever having played an instrument or learned how to read music before my 21st birthday. If I were tasked with developing a career development class, this would be a perfect story to use.

6. Encourage practice and repetition. According to Malcolm Gladwell's 2011 book, *Outliers*, if you practice anything for 10,000 hours you'll be considered an expert both by demonstrated knowledge and ability. Clearly, this is an impractical concept in this setting, but the point is well taken. Practice and repetition pushes more data into long-term memory.

THE BRAIN/BODY CONNECTION

A common misunderstanding about the brain and the body is that they operate independently from each other. In reality, one is an extension, or perhaps more accurately a reflection, of the other. For example, recent biomedical research has demonstrated that a delicate balance exists between the immune system and the stress response.[10] Cortisol, a powerful hormonal byproduct of stress is also a powerful immune-cell inhibitor. This begs the fundamental question, "What is stress?" It is simply a perception of an event that has occurred, is occurring, or might occur. So, then what is a perception? It is a thought. Deepak Chopra says it best, "Our immune system is constantly eavesdropping on our internal dialogue." Our thoughts can actually be linked to illness. For example, stress is a risk factor for heart disease. This is a powerful example of the brain/body connection at work, of the brain having a profound effect on the body.

Conversely, it was always thought that the nerve cells or neurons you were born with were all you were going to get. We now know that through a process called neurogenesis, new nerve cells have been shown to grow in the hippocampus region and subventricular zone of the brain. How? One prominent way is through aerobic activity. Exercise gives life to new neurons, and environmental interaction helps them to survive. Aerobic activity brings many benefits to the brain, but neurogenesis is one striking example of how the body impacts the brain.

In his book *SPARK: The Revolutionary New Science of Exercise and the Brain*, John Ratey, Harvard associate clinical professor of psychiatry, says that exercise is like "Miracle-Gro" for the brain.[11] In other words, researchers are piling up more evidence that one of the main beneficiaries of aerobic exercise is the brain—Wow!

Ongoing research in this area focuses on physical fitness and academic achievement and also on how acute bouts of aerobic activity impact cognitive function. A recent study in the *Journal of Abnormal Child Psychology* concluded that students in exercise groups showed greater improvements in attention and mood than their sedentary counterparts. Another recent study from the University of Eastern Finland reported a link between higher levels of physical activity at recess and better reading skills.

Recognition of the brain/body connection is crucial to your overall view of using movement as a tool in training. Understanding that "learning doesn't happen from the neck up, but from the feet up" gives a broader perspective to the teaching and learning process. On a personal level, the more you understand about the brain/body connection, the more you can impact "it" rather than always being an unknowing slave to its will. What you think matters. What you do and how much you move matters.

IMPLICATION FOR TRAINING

The implication for trainers is that paying attention to what your participants think, eat, drink, and do is a perfectly appropriate focus if you want to increase the effectiveness of training events. Of course, you can't control what participants do outside your class, but while they are in your class keeping stress under control and ensuring proper blood flow is certainly within your purview.

To accomplish these goals, begin by asking the right questions.

- What is the "state" (brain/body emotional state) of the participants when they enter class and how will I effectively manage or change this "state"?
- How can I make a positive impact on the participants' readiness to learn?

■ How can I insert movement and use of the body into the training design?

Training Design with the Brain in Mind

Your role as trainer is one of the key elements in design. Shifting your self-view from "trainer" to "facilitator of learning" and "designer of the learning environment" provides a whole new perspective on the teaching and learning process. It allows for different kinds of decisions to be made with regard to how often to move, the specific reason for movement, and how the brain would prefer to interact with this content. Learning often happens apart from the trainer. Your job is to facilitate and/or design effective training. Sometimes that means direct instruction/lecture, but often it means being creative and doing everything possible to create powerful rehearsal of material.

Tell Them What You Told Them

If you want to make sure your audience remembers what you want them to remember about your presentation, the familiar training and presentation admonition to state the most important points twice, once at the beginning and again at the end of your presentation, is a research-backed fact.[13]

But why does this technique work? Basically, at the beginning of a learning event our learners have plenty of working memory space, but as soon as the session starts, the space quickly fills up and everything after this overload occurs is often lost. You can avoid this overload by allowing time for rehearsal, chunking, and storage, thus creating additional working memory capacity. It's important to remember, however, that rehearsal, chunking, and storage time must be increased in direct proportion to the length of the training segment. The length of this process varies with the type and amount of content and individual learning needs.

The big picture is that learning episodes should be kept to a minimum with frequent opportunities for rehearsal of the new information, movement to create an efficient and energized trainee, and frequent interaction with other participants.

Designing a two-hour or two-day training session takes careful thought if you want to incorporate some of the brain-based research techniques discussed in this chapter. To help you get started, here are some critical concepts to explore in key areas that impact the success of your learning event.

- **Physical Environment.** Is the training space and environment conducive for learning? Is the space well lit and at an acceptable temperature, spacious enough for movement, and easy to reconfigure and transition to facilitate group interaction?

- **Emotional Environment.** How will you create a safe and emotionally positive environment to facilitate risk-taking? How will you gain the brain's attention and make use of novelty from the start of the session? Can you create training event-rich content that will allow learners to have "ah-ha" moments that make learning stick? What techniques will you use to manage the brain/body states of the trainees?

- **Content Delivery and Facilitation.** Considering the memory limitations of your learners, how will you make the best and most efficient use of the time available? How can learning be divided and chunked in ways that won't overwhelm working memory, yet will provide ample time for practice and rehearsal? What movement strategies will you use so trainees are ready to learn? How will you keep learners alert and feeling connected to one another to encourage learning? How will you design learning that accommodates all learning styles of the participants? How will you make information relevant and meaningful?

■ **Teach to the Whole Brain.** Design training that appeals not only to people who are auditory preferred, verbal-linguistic, logical, or highly organized, but also to those who see the big picture or are more creative, kinesthetic or spontaneous.

KEY CONCEPTS

■ Shift your self-view from "trainer" to the "facilitator/designer." Learning often happens apart from the trainer. Your job is to facilitate and/or design effective training. Sometimes that means direct instruction/lecture, but often it means being creative and doing everything possible to create powerful rehearsal of material.

■ Shorter learning segments are better because our brain's temporary memory storage is limited. Keep direct learning episodes and lectures to less than 30 minutes to avoid tiring out your learners' brains. The brain needs practice and rehearsal of information (which is unique to the learner) so it can process and retain information for later use. Use novelty to gain the brain's attention throughout training. Subtle ways of achieving this include changing voice inflection or facilitating from different areas of the room. More obvious use of novelty includes the use of movement, music, or a brain teaser related to the activity or concept you want/need your learners to grasp.

■ Make sure learning is relevant and meaningful as a strategy to ensure that content is stored in long-term memory. Regularly remind participants how the information you are presenting will be useful or ask participants to complete interest inventories prior to training that you can use as part of training design.

■ Create a positive learning environment that plays to our brain's need for safety. A safe environment means your participants are more likely to take risks and be more engaged in learning. Safety is often demonstrated through appropriate ice-breakers, positive language, and feedback, playing music before training begins, or designing an initial fun and engaging activity.

■ Include plenty of learner interaction throughout a training event. Discussion helps trainees create sense and meaning—relevance to a learner's previous experiences—and this connection helps participants permanently store information. Carefully monitor and if necessary control discussions so that no single participant dominates.

■ "Read" your audience by observing participant body language and be a good "state-manager" (trainer-directed management of a learner's brain/body emotional state). You can accomplish this by using plenty of movement and novelty throughout the training. The longer a learner sits, the more likely it is that his or her attention will waver. Movement circulates blood flow to the brain and reenergizes the learner.

■ Make learning "real" in the training design. Create real learning situations and give relatable examples. Avoid long lectures or the reading of PowerPoint slide bullets.

■ In general, anything you still remember the next day has a strong chance of being stored in permanent memory. That's because sleep serves as the brain's "off-line" switch, and this down time allows the hippocampus to encode new information into permanent memory.

EIGHT BRAIN PRINCIPLES WORKSHEET

This chapter discussed eight key ways that our brains prefer to receive, process, and store information. Review each of the preferences cited and jot down how you currently use or plan to use these principles in your learning events.

Learning Preference	Currently Use	Plan to Use	How will you incorporate these learning preferences into current and future training programs?
Our brain is preprogramed to notice novelty in the surrounding environment. Changing up the environment resets this innate scanning switch and allows for focused attention from your learners.			
Learning and movement are innately connected in the human brain. That's why learning new concepts and taking in new information through the use of our bodies is one of the most effective learning technologies available to trainers. It's all about implicit learning—the brain's preferred way to learn.			
Learning is enhanced when we connect and communicate with others. Managing this basic need for connection and community in your classroom will increase the likelihood that more of the information you present will be stored in long-term memory and retained for later use.			
Emotional connection enhances the learning experience. If a strong enough emotion is detected, the amygdala may encode the memory with an emotional tag.			

(*continues*)

Learning Preference	Currently Use	Plan to Use	How will you incorporate these learning preferences into current and future training programs?
Learn by doing is a fundamental learning preference. The most effective training is hands-on, concrete, and directly applicable to what actions are required to produce the desirable outcome.			
Connecting new knowledge to old knowledge improves retention. Our brains are wired to make this connection, and we feel good when we connect the new information with the old.			
Down time is required to ensure new learning is processed and stored. Short bursts of content should be followed by review, practice, and rehearsal activity to provide the opportunity for information to be transferred to the permanent memory lock box and is supported by repetition and time away from learning activities. A retention check (in a multiday learning event) should be done the next day to make sure sleep has done its job to firmly cement the content in long-term memory.			
Down time is required to ensure new learning is processed and stored. A low-stress, highly engaging environment works best to encourage learning.			

Notes

1. Oberparleiter, L. (2004). *Brain-Based Teaching and Learning.* Department of Education, Gratz College. Graduate Course Trainers Manual. Randolph, NJ: Center for Lifelong Learning.
2. Sousa, D. (2011). *How the Brain Learns.* Thousand Oaks, CA: Corwin.
3. *Ibid.*
4. *Ibid.*
5. *Ibid.*
6. Oberparleiter.
7. Sprenger, M. (1999). *Learning and Memory: The Brain in Action.* Alexandria, VA: Association for Supervision and Curriculum Development.
8. *Ibid.*
9. Sousa.
10. Sternberg, E. & Gold, P. (2002). The mind-body interaction in disease: The hidden mind. (Special Edition). *Scientific American,* 12(1), 82–129.
11. Ratey, J. (2008). SPARK: *The Revolutionary New Science of Exercise and the Brain.* New York: Little Brown.
12. *Ibid.*
13. Sousa.

CHAPTER 3

Applying the Benefits of Movement

We all have an innate need to move. That's why we don't like any activity or circumstance that forces us to sit, stand or interact statically with our environment. As children we dealt with the stress and frustration of confinement by "fidgeting;" now, as fully realized adults we still "fidget" and "squirm" to deal with inertia but in more socially accepted ways such as "fidgeting" endlessly with our smart phones during moments of inactivity, though pen and finger tapping, doodling, drawing, and talking are still commonplace.

> *Your brain works better on the move. There's no time like the present.*
> James A. Levine, M.D., Ph.D., Professor of Endocrinology and
> Nutrition Research at Mayo Clinic, author of *The Blue Notebook*

Of course, this phenomenon is old news to trainers or anyone else whose livelihood depends on how well they engage the attention of other people. And while we do our best to engage our innately restless participants, we know it's just not possible to engage everyone, and so we just accept the loss of a few participants during every training event.

But is this audience "loss" as inevitable as we believe? What if you could turn an assumed training liability—our "gotta' move" tendencies—into a learning asset that could potentially engage any audience while at the same time increase their retention levels? Let me illustrate this promise with a recent experience every trainer or facilitator would recognize as the perfect set up for a learning disaster.

WORST OF TIMES

I was working with group of adults recently who made it clear they were not delighted by the prospect of participating in a Friday afternoon training session. This is not such an unusual situation, so I did my best to position the topic in a positive a way. I thought I was doing fine until a participant asked the single most important question on everyone's mind:

"So are we getting out of here this afternoon . . . at 3 or at 4 pm?"

"Closer to 4," I answered without hesitation, immediately regretting the quick, specific answer.

Suddenly, I felt hope and possibility rush out of the room like a departing spirit and a palpable sense of hopelessness and desperation replace it. If you had stood with me that day, it would have been hard to imagine I could do anything to save the class short of passing out $100 bills to every participant.

Yet within 30 minutes of starting the class, the most reluctant and disengaged learner—you know the one, slouching, mumbling, unprepared, nearly hostile—had been transformed into the most engaged and commutative learner in the room. And the rest of the learners had fallen in line. Everyone was focused on learning. Everyone was laughing and having fun all the while absorbing the content that they had been sent to learn.

This transformation didn't require "supertrainer" skills or any special talent beyond the skills all good learning professionals develop through experience. Like so many learning success stories, all that's really needed to duplicate these results are a few simple tools and a little guidance on how to use them. To prove my point, I've included a detailed account at the end of this chapter describing how these amazing results were achieved.

WHAT TRAINERS SHOULD DO

So, how do trainers and other learning professionals engage such a potentially distracted audience? Yes, it's a challenge, but here's what I know about keeping audiences of all types engaged by using movement, whether the format is time-intensive, multiday training, professional development facilitation or presentations at a conference.

- Adults generally need to move at least once an hour, if not more often. Here is a paradigm shift. Think of standing as the norm and sitting as the "when necessary" position. Just because culturally "sitting" has been deemed "normal" doesn't make it best for learning or even the most healthy. Based on the brain/body connection, and as previously mentioned, "learning doesn't happen from neck up, it happens from the feet up." As facilitators of learning and designers of the learning environment, that statement should help frame how often adults should be moving. Also, consider the following factors:
  - **Time of Day.** For most learners, attention span decreases and cognitive function declines as the day moves along

and they tire. That's why movement is even more necessary later in the day, especially in the afternoon.

○ **Type of Activity.** Is the activity a lecture or discussion or something sedentary like watching a video or a peer coaching and/or role-play exercise?

○ **Energy Level Created by the Facilitator.** How engaged is the facilitator with the content and presentation style? Is the facilitator engaging, energetic and on top of his or her game?

It is the trainer's responsibility to create engaging training environments that motivate and challenge learners. Movement is just one more tool you can use to strengthen your learner's ability to pay attention and improve cognitive abilities. Here's an example to illustrate the point that even small changes can make a big difference in learning.

LEARNING THAT ENGAGES

Successful learning begins by keeping the end goal in mind—that is, finding a way to ensure that training participants recall and use the information or content you present. We know this noble goal is not 100 percent achievable, as the brain simply isn't set up to remember every conscious experience, but training programs should begin with this goal in mind.

So why does more movement lead to more learning? The answer to this question is both simple and complex. The simple answer is that movement helps us refocus our "fidgeting" brains by increasing oxygen and blood flow to the brain. The more complex answer, which is that movement changes our brain chemistry so that we're more alert, positive, and accepting of learning, is the more difficult avenue to explore. The neuroscience behind it is beyond the scope of this book, but if readers are curious to know more, additional re-sources are included in the bibliography. However, the eight key ways that movement enhances the learning process offered below try to strike a reasonable and useful balance between the two extremes.

EIGHT WAYS MOVEMENT ENHANCES THE TRAINING PROCESS

1. **Movement Creates Pathways for Implicit Learning.** Implicit learning is generally defined as learning that takes place beyond our conscious awareness. It's the difference between learning how to do something like replacing a light bulb by watching someone else do it and by reading a precise and detailed technical description of how to change a light bulb. Sure, the second will still enable you to change the light bulb, but the process would take longer and create a great deal of anxiety. Training often relies on explicit channels, such as PowerPoint slides, discussion, exercises, and memorization. Unfortunately, these methods don't align with the brain's preferred learning pathways. Though there are many ways for implicit learning to take place, movement is an exceptionally strong implicit learning tool. Too often irrelevant content that's beyond the learner's interest is force fed through overloaded pathways, such as discussion and presentation, workbook exercises, or rote memorization. These methods are not efficient nor are they the brain's preferred pathways for retention.

> Here's an example I often use in my classes.
> First, I ask participants if they can name the first ten presidents of the United States. No matter the audience size or

education level, very few participants can answer this question. That's understandable since the only way someone might retain this information would be through rote memorization or perhaps repeated exposure to the list through an explicit learning channel.

Next, I ask the audience, "Who can change a light bulb?" All the participants raise their hands. I explain that this expert knowledge was acquired through direct experiential learning and that our brains really prefer to learn in this way. To make my point, I challenge the participants to imagine learning the same skill by following a set of written instructions. Of course, this is not to say all learning should use our implicit, "learn-by-doing" channel. On the contrary, the most powerful learning occurs when implicit and explicit learning experiences are blended (or perhaps more precisely, allowed to work in concert).

For example, assume you're tasked with explaining a difficult concept, such as how the brain instructs the human body to produce coordinated movement in our arms and legs. You could offer a 30-minute explanation of the neurological and chemical processes that make this miracle happen. Or, you could directly tie each specific process associated with movement to an arm or leg movement you ask the participants to perform.

Clearly, the first technical presentation offers a great deal of excellent content. Unfortunately, few learners will find the content engaging and even fewer will recall anything you've told them. On the other hand, using both implicit and explicit techniques (movement in concert with content delivery) produces engaged learners who have greater content recall and better application on the job.

2. **Movement Refocuses Attention and Provides a Break From Learning.** Working memory in our brain is similar to a computer's RAM in that both have limited capacity. Trainers often overload our brain's working memory (three-to-five items of unrelated bits of information) and don't allow time for processing and storing information. That's why shorter bits of information are better. Movement refocuses participant attention, and this can help the brain store new information and prepare it to receive new content. This is especially true if the brain is working to process new information with little relevance to the learner. Imagine working memory as a small paper cup that only holds so much water. When it's full, the cup overflows and the excess water is lost. The area of the brain that houses the equivalent of a computer's RAM is the frontal lobe, but this important work is only one of the frontal lobe's functions. Still, it's important to know where this activity takes place.

   Movement increases the efficiency of the process by providing learners a "second wind" of refocused attentiveness. You can achieve this attention refreshment results in many ways, but I often use "brain breaks" (short bursts of physical activity) to increase blood flow in the body and brain. This creates a more efficient learner and learning environment.

   You'll find numerous examples of these "breaks" later in the book, but a brain break can be as simple as asking learners to find a partner to discuss the three major points you've just presented in class. It's not a sophisticated technique, but I'm always surprised by the refocusing and retention results that occur when learners move their bodies and interact with other learners during any movement activity.

3. **Movement Creates Motivation.** Movement promotes five key human needs that underpin human motivation. The re-

searcher William Glasser (1998) identified these needs as part of his choice theory and internal control psychology.[1] Glasser's five basic human needs include:

· Survival
· Belonging
· Power
· Freedom
· Fun

These needs are not often addressed in training settings, but when these conditions are met through movement, motivation is the natural result. After all, humans are naturally drawn toward connection, competence, choice, enjoyment, and safety.[2] Kinesthetic learning experiences, or using movement in different contexts in teaching, training, and learning, encourages these optimal learning states for learners. The need to belong is easily met since many kinesthetic activities are done in pairs or groups. Training effectiveness and using the body to learn or remember a concept meets the need for power or "competence" through engaging more ways that learners naturally learn. Finally, fun is most often a natural byproduct of movement and is easily provided for during training that engages the brain and body. Glasser discusses the fact that fun is a natural payoff for learning. It is my assertion that movement makes learning more brain compatible and easier to come by thus creating a more motivated learner and learning environment.

4. **Movement Improves the Learning State.** A positive learning state occurs when a participant's emotional state, that is, interest and focus on the topic, and physical state, that is, a feeling of hunger or discomfort, is balanced. Balance means that the participant is focused, engaged, and comfortable. Trainers should be keenly aware of when these states are out

of balance and actively work to correct this imbalance. Simply observing whether or not the participants are tired, uncomfortable, or bored is a simple recognition that plays an important role in a trainer's professional success. A learner with a positive learning state has a greater potential to understand and retain the concepts and information presented. The brain/body emotional state is also connected to long-term memory storage. Sousa indicates that meaning and sense are two nonnegotiable criteria for content retention.[3] Of the two, meaning is the more powerful, and meaning making is state dependent—a critical brain/body component that is often overlooked by trainers. Thus, the learner's positive emotional state increases the likelihood that meaning will be found in the learning and long-term storage of content will more likely occur. I put movement in the category of being a powerful force to manage learning state. Here's a scenario to explain the concept.

Imagine that you've got a room full of learners and it's been an hour since the last official break. For the last few minutes you've noticed a slow drain of energy from the room, but you decide to soldier on despite your sense that the participants are hungry and tired of sitting. Here's where a brain break would be helpful, even a break as simple as allowing learners to stand and stretch would likely save the day and a restore a positive learning state.

5. **Movement Differentiates Training.** Over the past decade, school-age students have become accustomed to something called "differentiated instruction." Instead of a one-size fits all type of instruction (that may be the norm for many mature trainees), differentiation focuses on the diverse needs of all learners in your class. These same students are now entering our corporate training classes, so it's essential to adjust

training practices to accommodate more "active" learning styles by incorporating more movement-based "doing" and "seeing" techniques into your training programs. Differentiation of learning styles is a complex teaching challenge, but assuming that a good number of your learners prefer visual and kinesthetic learning, the challenge must be faced for optimal results. The differences in learning style, readiness, interest, and culture that are present in most, if not all training, make a "one-size-fits-all" type of training outdated.

6. **Movement Engages the Senses.** Our brains crave sensory cues, such as listening, writing, watching, hearing, and discussing to facilitate the learning process. Movement adds another layer to the learning senses and, in particular, helps engage the senses that contribute most to learning, which are seeing, hearing, and touching.

7. **Movement Reduces Stress.** Movement produces dopamine in our brains, often called the feel-good hormone. It is associated with movement, pleasure, mood, sleep, and working memory. The production of this hormone reduces stress, and less stress means more learning potential for participants through the use of their bodies and movement. Adding movement to the learning experience just increases the odds that learners will retain and store the information you present. One learning researcher even ranks the learning potential of movement on par with the senses of sight, hearing and touch.[4]

Using movement as part of an integrated training experience serves to foster a positive training environment. The result is a learning environment that minimizes stress while maximizing learning.

8. **Movement Enhances Episodic Learning and Memory.** Our brains pay detailed attention to the learning conditions or

situations and associate them with specific learning or information. When movement is associated with a concept, a unique environmental note is made by the brain connecting the concept learned with the circumstances under which it was learned. This brain bookmark creates a reference point that makes later recall much easier. For example, your learners are more likely to remember the French word for nose *(nez)* if you write it on a whiteboard display and then asked learners to repeat the word while squeezing their noses.

ATTENTION SPAN AND TRAINING

Adults have a remarkably short attention spans—about 15 to 20 minutes according to most researchers.[5] But that statistic does not consider context, that is, whether the adult is in a typical office meeting or engaged in a group activity with a specific purpose. Emotional state is also not likely part of this attention calculation. Still, the fact remains that trainers must do everything possible to use their audiences short focus time to engage them and transfer as much knowledge as possible to their long-term memories. This job is not made any easier by all the convenient and entertaining distractions (including negative emotional distractions and mobile computing devices) inside and outside the classroom.

Unfortunately, short of collecting smart phones and iPads at the beginning of a class, this is likely a permanent distraction. Frankly, it might be more distracting to collect these devices since your learners would be more distracted worrying about all the emails or important calls and texts they're missing.

After more than a decade of teaching graduate education courses in a time-intensive format (a series of single or multiday events), here is what I consider the top three "must haves" to create powerful and engaging learning experiences.

1. The training design must be spot on, near perfect, and well tested.
2. The instructor must have done at least 50 hours of training and be skilled at working with adults in a time-intensive format.
3. Movement, either built into the course design or instructor dependent, must be included in the training.

Deciding when and how to include movement requires a keen awareness of the audience's mood. Here are some questions to ask when making this determination:

- What does your instinct tell you about the mood of the room?
- What have previous trainings shown you about the attention span of your trainees?
- What appears to be the attention span of trainees when they are not interested in the topic or PowerPoint presentation or lecture?
- How much material can I truly cover and still have trainees comprehend, process, and retain the information?
- Are you aware of any particular individuals who prefer to move or are kinesthetic in nature (former athletes, dancers, performers, and those who prefer to move around the office as opposed to sitting for long periods of time)?

WHAT MOVEMENT CAN ACCOMPLISH

A CEO of a signage company once called me to consult with his team in preparation for a very important presentation. The company was facing a critical point in the contracting process of a potential client (the company was one of three finalists), and the CEO wanted to give his company the best shot possible. During a run through of the final presentation, I learned that the client was scheduled to make their pitch at noon, not really an optimal time slot. As a general rule, people have started to think about lunch.

To counteract this time disadvantage, I suggested a strategy that would require the selection committee members to stand up and move during his company's presentation. I explained the reasons for my suggestion—using the same justifications presented in this book. We developed a plan that required the selection committee to stand behind their chairs, pass around samples of my client's signage, and then move their bodies to track the presenting CEO as he circulated about the room.

My client not only won the contract because it was judged the best company for the job for a variety of reasons, including technical ability and customer service, but also because of its enthusiasm and innovation in presentation. It's also not hard to imagine a different outcome had the committee members been thinking about lunch or how sleepy they were.

FOUR PURPOSES OF MOVEMENT IN TRAINING

The story of the CEO's success in engaging his audience through movement illustrates a useful application of this book's major principles. But how might training professionals incorporate movement into the work they do day in and out? Here are four distinct techniques to focus on.

Purpose 1: Reenergize the Brain and Body

Brain breaks are multipurpose activities that serve as important learning state management tools in reenergizing the brain and body.

Trainers often cover too much content to stay on schedule and cover required material. While having learners in their seats might seem the most efficient way to accomplish this goal, it's actually counter-productive. That's because our bodies crave a regular infusion of fresh oxygen. Without it, our ability to concentrate and focus plummets, resulting in bored, slumping learners, which are a sure sign of working memory overload. By introducing brain breaks, you'll accomplish the following:

- A reinvigorated and energized learning state.
- Increased blood flow around the brain and body, and thus increased focus.
- The introduction of humor through laughter and fun—into training has its own learning rewards.

Purpose 2: Team Building

Team building is encouraged when learners are relaxed and willing to take risks through active engagement in discussions or interacting in a positive way with other learners. Movement improves communication, builds relationships, and strengthens critical thinking skills.

Every successful business relies on collaborative and cooperative teams. One of the benefits of movement-oriented activities is that certain key baseline emotional needs are met through participation. If this need is not met, the part of the brain involved in higher level critical thinking skills strategies shuts down and team dynamics suffer.[6]

Emotional climate is also a key component for learning new information. When participants feel comfortable taking risks, they participate in more group discussions. Here are some benefits of using movement activities to build teams:

- Improves communication and builds risk-taking relationships.
- Builds problem-solving, critical, and higher-level thinking skills.
- Motivates by meeting basic human need of belonging.
- Brings enjoyment that benefits both participant's brains and bodies.

Purpose 3: Review and Retention

Retention through practice (repeating a skill over time) and rehearsal (the reprocessing of information in working memory) is greatly enhanced if the participants are able to associate the desired learning with a movement that helps imbed the information kinesthetically. Just because information is presented to us one, two, or three times does not guarantee the information will make a lasting impression on the brain. This maxim is especially true if the information is not relevant, meaningful, or emotionally engaging.

Yes, repeating or writing something 500 times does work to sear information into our brains, but this is a very inefficient way to learn. Movement provides a framework for training content review while enhancing practice and rehearsal, an activity that helps make information stick. Reviewing training content through movement provides:

- A brain break without taking a formal brain break.
- An opportunity to encourage engagement.
- A basis for motivation.
- An opportunity for repetition that improves retention.

Purpose 4: Effective Training

Information acquired during a movement activity does stick, but movement cannot be incorporated into every learning program or content area. So how do you determine if movement is an appropriate learning tool to use? In most cases, the answer is as obvious as deter-mining whether tennis should be taught by lecture or by doing. Learning by doing helps make learning stick and leads to effective training by connecting the needs of both the body and the brain. The technique is especially effective for new learning.

Using implicit learning techniques means that:

- More information is stored in long-term memory.
- Learning is more tangible when a brain and body connection is added.

DECIDING WHEN TO USE MOVEMENT

Movement is not meant to replace training techniques in all circum-stances. In many cases, movement is a good choice when training a new concept since physical movement stores information more effi-ciently and enhances recall. Still, no formula exists per se, and the choice ultimately falls to your instincts and experience as a profes-sional trainer.

There have been times when I've noticed the energy of the learn-ers waning in a way (stretching, yawning, not paying attention) that indicates the need to reenergized. Clearly, a brain break is in order. Yet other times I've come across a "movable moment," where some piece of content could be easily taught through the use of move-ment. I have always chosen this route over lecture, as I am quite fa-miliar with the retention rate of both. A decision to use movement can also be planned well in advance. The advantage is an activity that can be well planned and practiced to ensure its success. Begin experimenting with movement by incorporating simple brain breaks to build your confidence. Then, move on to more difficult activities, including reviewing and teaching content.

REST OF THE STORY

Unfortunately, many training designs still attempt to bludgeon content into the participant's brains with PowerPoint bullets. Note that I took exactly the opposite approach in the previous example, in which I delivered information in short, relevant bursts coupled with activities focused squarely on the needs of learner's brains. It was a deliberate strategy that resulted in learner interest, motivation, engagement and, best of all, content recall.

So now that you know a little more about using movement in training, here is how I used these principles to engage the group of reluctant learners I faced in the scenario at the beginning of this chapter. This exercise took about 30 minutes to complete. Since the topic of the training was to demonstrate how motivation and the brain are connected, the movement I used effectively showed connection.

1. First, I provided a five-minute personal introduction that included a funny, but true, story pertinent to the training. (Personal Engagement; Emotional Connection; Relationship Building with Audience)
2. Then, I facilitated a specific partnering activity that provided periodic movement with different partners as a way for the participants to engage and learn the new content. It's important for learners to have ample opportunity to make sense of what they've learned through discussion and to build personal relevancy to the material. (This will be discussed in greater depth later in the book.)
3. Next, I asked the partnered pairs to do two tasks within a specified timeframe:
   a) Describe your family to your partner.

b) Describe something that you did or accomplished that was a source of pride. (Building Relationships Among Trainees)

4. Next, the entire group of partnered participants gathered together and participated in an activity called "TV Themes." I asked the participants to listen to audio clips of 20 different TV themes (about 30 seconds each). Then, each of the partnered pairs worked together to write down as many of the TV themes they could remember. (This was a lesson in working memory capacity, emotional engagement, and, again, the importance of building relationships). I'm very careful about using this activity based on audience make-up. People of different ages, backgrounds, and cultures have their own unique history with television. It worked very well in this scenario.

5. Finally, I asked the group to gather the chairs in a circle. I asked one participant to describe something he or she enjoyed doing (for example, hiking or traveling). Then, all the participants who enjoyed the same activity were instructed to get up and find another seat in the circle. Once the participants were settled in their new seats, the next participant (to the right of the first respondent) stated a new "like," and the process was repeated.

The group was thoroughly motivated, engaged, and excited to learn more after doing these exercises. I simply went back to the originally planned training and discussed the brain basis for each of the activities we had just completed.

The training that followed was lively and engaged. The exercise allowed the participants to connect information on state management, the importance of emotion in learning and memory formation, the limits of working memory, and the fundamentals of motivating others through relationship building, an essential prerequisite that leads to information being stored in the brain's long-term memory.

KEY CONCEPTS

- ■ Movement enhances training in eight different ways, including increasing implicit learning opportunities, refocusing attention and providing a break from learning, inspiring motivation, improving the learning state, differentiating training, engaging the senses, reducing stress, and increasing episodic learning opportunities.

- ■ Movement is not only appropriate in training but in meeting facilitation, sales presentation, and conference presentation.

- ■ There are four purposes of using movement in a training scenario. They include (1) reenergizing the brain and body, (2) team building, (3) review and retention and (4) effective training.

BENEFITS OF MOVEMENT WORKSHEET

The magic of movement is very real because it changes the brain in ways that enhance the learning process in eight specific ways. Based on your reading of this chapter, makes some notes about how you might incorporate movement benefits into your own training programs. As you work through the book, pay particular attention to additional information, tips, or techniques that will help meet these needs and jot down some notes on why this benefit is currently so important.

Benefit of Movement	How will you incorporate these movement principles into current and future training programs?
Allows for Implicit Learning Implicit learning takes place beyond our conscious awareness. Training often relies on explicit channels, such as PowerPoint slides, discussion, exercises, and memorization, but these methods don't align with the brain's preferred pathways. It's the difference between learning how to do something like replace a light bulb by watching it done and then doing it yourself and reading a precise and detailed description about how to do it.	
Provides a Break and Refocuses Attention Working memory (akin to a computer's RAM) has limited capacity for retention. Training often overloads our brain's RAM without allowing time for processing and storing information. That's why shorter bits of information are better. Movement refocuses participant attention to allow time for the brain to store new information and prepare it to receive new content.	
Creates Motivation Movement promotes five key human needs that underpin human motivation: survival, belonging, power, freedom, and fun. Training participants who have these needs met are more motivated learners.	

Benefit of Movement	How will you incorporate these movement principles into current and future training programs?
Improves the Learning State Participants develop a positive learning state, in which a balance exists between a participant's emotional state (interest and focus on the topic) and physical state (hungry and uncomfortable). Trainers should be keenly aware when these states are out of balance.	
Differentiates Training The most effective trainers do their best to accommodate the different learning styles favored by participants, but such accommodation is not always possible. That's why the introduction is so important. It offers a well-documented avenue for learning.	
Engages the Senses Our brains crave sensory cues, such as listening, writing, watching, hearing, and discussing, to facilitate the learning process. Movement adds another layer to the learning senses and in particular adds strength to the powerful senses that contribute most to learning—seeing, hearing, and touching.	
Reduces Stress Movement produces dopamine in our brains, often called the feel-good hormone. The production of this hormone reduces stress, and less stress means more learning potential for participants.	
Enhances Episodic Learning and Memory Information is easier to recall when it's paired with a dynamic experience, so that concepts linked to movement make them easier to recall when needed.	

Notes

1. Glasser, W. (1998). *Choice Theory: A New Psychology for Personal Freedom*. New York: HarperCollins.
2. Sullo, B. (2007). *Activating the Desire to Learn*. Alexandria, VA: Association for Supervision and Curriculum Development.
3. Sousa, D. (2011). *How the Brain Learns*. Thousand Oaks, CA: Corwin.
4. Sousa.
5. Sousa.
6. Lengel, T. & Kuczala, M. (2010) *The Kinesthetic Classroom: Teaching and Learning through Movement*. Thousand Oaks, CA: Corwin.

Movement Activities for Training

- Chapter 4—Brain-Break Activities
- Chapter 5—Team-Building Activities
- Chapter 6—Content-Review Activities

Section 2 offers a range of movement-based activities that will help your learners refocus their brains and prepare for new learning, build emotional connection to other learners and their organizations that build learning capacity, and review content in fun and playful ways that encourage long-term retention.

CHAPTER 4

Brain-Break Activities

Even before sophisticated technology allowed us to understand exactly how our brains get overloaded with information, we knew from experience that a little time was required for our brains to process and store newly acquired knowledge. So it's surprising how many trainers and other learning professionals still sometimes follow instructional models that don't take advantage of these known facts about how our brains function.

Sometimes the reason for this default to less efficient methods is that the content is tied to mandated coverage required by corporate and regulatory directives that box trainers into strict time restraints to present all the necessary learning. And, while these real-world dynamics do exist, that doesn't always offer trainers a free pass to ignore the effective brain-based techniques presented in this chapter. This is especially true, if using these techniques will increase the odds that learners will remember more of what they were intended (or mandated) to learn and, importantly, use back on the job.

> *As far as the brain is concerned, shorter is usually better. . . .*
>
> Mike Kuczala

THE GOALS OF A BRAIN BREAK

A brain break does just what it says; it gives the brain a break to help prevent working memory overload. This helps the process of preparing new information before the most relevant content is passed along to long-term memory for later recall. As you discovered in previous chapters, the brain's central processing center for this activity is called the hippocampus. You'll also recall that unless something happens to this information—usually in the form of practice or rehearsal—this conversion to long-term memory is unlikely to happen. Brain breaks are an essential training tool for every trainer. After all, the ultimate goal of training is knowledge recall and application in ways that improve job performance and increase business productivity.

Brain breaks also provide a much needed respite from sitting. Blood pools in the butt and legs, and brain breaks provide an opportunity to move blood and fresh oxygen around the brain and body, thereby reenergizing and refocusing learners. At the end of a brain break, you'll have a more energized and efficient group of learners who are better able to deal with training content. These breaks are simple yet powerful tools that are necessary for effective training.

A word about extending sitting. More and more research is showing up about the health detriments of sitting.[1] Extended sitting has been linked to higher rates of colon, endometrial, and lung cancer. Dr. James Levine, Director of the Mayo Clinic Arizona State University Obesity and Solutions Initiative, was quoted in a 2014 article in *Time* magazine, "Sitting Is Killing You": "In the same way that standing up is an oddity now, sitting down should be." All people, especially learners, should be standing much more than we ever thought for varying reasons.

HOW BRAIN BREAKS WORK

Brain breaks increase blood flow to the participant's bodies and brains. This increased supply of oxygen results in refreshed, refocused, and reenergized learners (this is the true value of a brain break). It's that simple. Over the years, I've heard a whole range of reactions from learners who were very happy for the opportunity to "just move" during training. I have even heard the word "magical." That's not really an overstatement of what these brain breaks can accomplish. Remember, the whole purpose of using a brain break is to manage participants' physiological and psychological states to help them be better learners. And yes, physiology can change psychology!

BRIDGING ENGAGEMENT BARRIERS

While brain breaks are an effective training tool, it does take a certain amount of confidence, even courage, to use them. Engagement barriers include your reluctance to use brain breaks or your trainees' reluctance to participate. If you are reluctant to use a brain break that you fear might seem "silly" to the participants—and by extension, make you look foolish—then be honest with your learners and invite them to relax any of their (and your) self-conscience adult barriers about looking foolish. This takes the "edge" off the activity. When I am in this situation, I usually just ask the participants a direct question, such as, "Will you be silly with me for a moment?" This usually diffuses most anxiety about the activity. It works for me as a trainer. You might want to say it in a different way. In addition, conveying that the activity will be fun or interesting can help.

After completing the activity, I ask the participants a series of questions that will help them recognize and use the change in their "state" (i.e., more relaxed, focused, and ready to work) to improve learning outcomes. Over time, this allows adult learners to feel and understand the importance of using brain breaks. Most likely, it will create an anticipation of their use on a regular basis. One idea to try is to use brain breaks regularly during multiday training. On the second or third day, provide no brain break. I guarantee you will be questioned about the missing brain break! A word of caution: You will undoubtedly have learners in your training sessions with physical disabilities, including those with limited mobility, visual, or auditory skills. Your judgment as a training professional will be your best guide as to how to handle the situation. Depending on whatever challenge is faced by your participant, I offer the following advice:

- Avoid certain activities altogether if that is most comfortable.
- Determine how the individual can participate safely and easily in an adapted way.

THE BEST TIME TO USE BRAIN BREAKS

Brain breaks are for the benefit of the learner to regroup, refocus, and reenergize. It is up to the trainer as the facilitator, designer, and professional to make decisions about when a brain break might best be utilized. In general, adult learners should be moving at least once per hour. These decisions will also be based on several key elements:

- What is the perceived learning state of the audience? Do the members seem tired, sluggish, or bored?
- Is there movement already planned that would take the place of a brain break, such as a team-building or discussion activity?

■ Have the participants recently finished eating? Can the content your trainees are working with not be interrupted?

These factors and others that you might discover all play a role in when brain breaks should be utilized. Most brain breaks produce the same result and play out in the same way, so differentiating between the activities for a desired result is likely unnecessary.

18 BRAIN-BREAK ACTIVITIES

Partnering is a commonly used training technique to reinforce content and concepts that rely on interaction, such as role play, to promote participant engagement and other training enrichment outcomes. My personal "go-to" partnering brain break is the "Time for a Partner" (see Figure 4.1).

1   Time for a Partner

Description   Participants partner with each other using an eight-segment (or another even number of your choosing) "clock" diagram that encourages connection with other participants. The connection device can be used to partner participants for any activity, including movement activities or to promote discussion between segment partners about any content having to do with the training. The point of the activity is to partner. How you use the partners is up to you as the trainer. I happen to use it mostly for discussion. If I've just made three critical points about the brain in one of my trainings, I might have particular partners discuss those three critical points for clarification, understanding, and meaning making. You could also use for something as simple as "find your three o'clock partner and give them a high five."

Materials Needed   Copies of the "Time for a Partner" template for each participant (see Figure 4.1) and extra pencils or pens.

Time   5-to-8 minutes depending on group size

Optimal Number of Participants   16 to 32

How to Conduct the Activity

- Pass out the partnering template to participants and explain the activity you plan to do with the partner clock. Explain that their job is to move around the room and pick a different partner for each of the clock's numbered segments. Encourage them to choose partners from outside their own area or table.

- When explaining the rules, remind participants that partnering is somewhat self-selecting. For example, if Dave asked

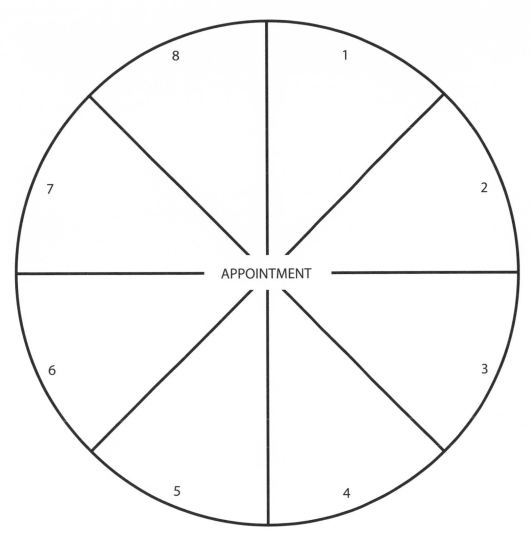

Figure 4.1 Time for a Partner

Mary to be his one o'clock partner, then Mary cannot ask someone else to be her one o'clock partner. The fact that Dave first asked Mary to be his partner means the Mary and Dave have both completed the partnering connection for the one o'clock segment.

- Tell the participants that once they have found a partner for a segment, each partner must sign the other's clock and move on to find a partner for another segment until all the segments are signed.

- In most cases, the partnering works out so that each person will have a page full of partners who have signed their clocks. If not, it's okay to put three participants together so the activity can be completed.

2   Famous Quotes

In addition to the appointment clock framework, I have used many other types of partnering with equally impressive results. One of my favorites involves the use of meaningful quotes from famous people. Here is a description of this activity.

Description   The activity is identical to the first brain break except that participants create partners using quotes instead of different numbers on a clock.

Materials Needed   Each participant should have a quote partners worksheet (see Figure 4.2) and a pen or pencil.

Time   5 to 8 minutes depending on group size

Optimal Number of Participants   16 to 32

How to Conduct the Activity

- Pass out the quote partner worksheet to participants and explain the activity you plan to do with it. For this activity, say that the participant's job is to move around the room and find a different partner for each one of the quotes listed on your worksheet. The result is still up to you. This can be used for partnering for any purpose, whether it be for high fives, discussion about content, or something else you've decided upon. The difference is that when you say "get together with quote partner #3, both partners will now have an inspirational quote to read to each other on meeting. It may provide inspiration or not. The point is that this is another way to create partners. Again, encourage them to choose partners from outside their own area or table.

- Tell the participants that each partner must sign the other's quote sheet and move on to finding a partner for the next quote.
- This worksheet can be changed as often as you like so as to use as many different quotes as you prefer.

SAMPLE QUOTE PARTNERS WORKSHEET

If you can dream it, you can do it.

Walt Disney, business magnate and animator

Partner #1 _____

Setting goals is the first step in turning the invisible into the visible.

Tony Robbins, life coach and self-help author

Partner #2 _____

You can never quit. Winners never quit, and quitters never win.

Ted Turner, media mogul and philanthropist

Partner #3 _____

If you've got a talent, protect it.

Jim Carrey, actor and comedian

Partner #4 _____

I'm intimidated by the fear of being average.

Taylor Swift, singer and songwriter

Partner #5 _____

Figure 4.2 Famous Quotes Handout

3 Walk'n'Talk

Description   Learners benefit from the opportunity to discuss or "unpack" what they've learned. This activity achieves two, perhaps three, important brain break goals. First, the activity involves movement which increases blood around the body and to the brain. Second, it clears working memory to make room for new information through practice and rehearsal. Finally, it creates personal meaning and relevance for the learner that also benefits the learning process.

Materials Needed   No special materials needed

Time   10 to 15 minutes

Optimal Number of Participants   As many as are in the training

How to Conduct the Activity

- Instruct participants to find a conveniently located partner (sitting close by, if possible).
- Next, instruct the partners to "take a walk" together outside the training space, if possible, but if the area is large enough to accommodate all the participants, it's okay to use the immediate area.
- Now ask the partners to discuss (while they are walking) pertinent details of previous learning or conduct a minibrainstorming session or any other collaboration method you wish to use.
- Set a very specific time frame and agenda for the exercise. When the participants return, choose a few of them to discuss what they talked about during their walk. (This step is optional.) The point of the walk is movement and a break for the participant's brain. You can use any variation of this activity you'd like to try since it works for almost any type of content.

4   1-2-3 Math!

Description   This activity is full of potential for laughter and fun and involves simple hand gestures and mathematical calculation.

Materials Needed   No special materials needed

Time   1 to 2 minutes

Optimal Number of Participants   From two up to as many are in the training

How to Conduct the Activity

- Instruct participants to find a partner. Mix up the method of choice so it goes beyond random choice or someone the participant knows. You can suggest choosing partners based on shirt color or birthday month or any other creative option. It adds to the fun.
- Once the partners are paired, ask each partner to simultaneously hit their own fist into the palm of their own hand three times. On what would be the fourth count, each partner should open their closed fist and show a random number of fingers between one and five to their partner.
- At this point, both partners are showing a particular number. For example, one partner might be showing "three fingers" and their partner might be showing "four fingers."
- Here is the point of the activity. While both partners are showing numbers, the first partner to add up the two numbers and shout out the total wins! In this case, the answer is seven.
- Partners should continue several more times at their own pace.
- This is not a group activity, but as the training leader you can make it more difficult and fun by changing the addition to

multiplication or subtraction during the activity or changing up the numbers and rules so that various mathematical combinations work for the game and the math abilities of the participants.

5   Finger Snatch

Description   This activity is also fast paced, so the competition creates a surge of adrenaline and cortisol for energy and focus. The activity is a classic "finger-grab" game that requires each pair of participants to stand opposite each other and hold out their hands. When the facilitator gives the signal, they attempt to "snatch" their opponent's index finger before it can be pulled away.

Materials Needed   No special materials needed

Time   1 to 2 minutes

Optimal Number of Participants   From two up to as many are in the training

How to Conduct the Activity

- Ask the participants to find a partner, again in some creative, logical or convenient way (such as a former partner or just the person sitting nearby).
- Ask the partners to face each other. Then, ask each of the partners to hold their right hands in front of them, palms ups.
- Next, instruct each of the partners to extend their left pointer finger and place the tip of the left pointer finger in the center of their partner's open right palm.
- Tell the participants that when you say "GO!," each of the partnered participants must simultaneously try to grab their partner's pointer finger before it can be pulled away while trying to pull their own pointer finger out of their partner's palm.
- It's not that easy. In fact, few are successful, so everyone gets a good laugh from this simple exercise.

6 Handshake and Fact

Description   This brain break uses a simple handshake to reinforce content, while providing movement that increases blood flow around the body to improve focus.

Materials Needed   No special materials needed

Time   10 to 15 minutes

Optimal Number of Participants   8 or more

How to Conduct the Activity

- Ask participants to stand. Then explain that this activity requires them to circulate randomly throughout the training space or facility and shake the hand of five other participants one at a time.
- Explain once they meet and shake the hand of another participant, the assignment is to review one fact or concept they've learned with their new acquaintance.
- Once the information has been exchanged, the meeting is over and the participant moves on to the next handshake and another discussion of a learned fact or concept gleaned from the training.
- Tell the participants to continue the handshake meetings and information exchange until they've met five different people.

7   Back-to-Back Low Five

Description   This brain break requires participants to stand back to back and swing their arms behind them to "low five" each other as many times as they can during a 30-second timeframe.

Materials Needed   A stopwatch or access to a watch with a second hand

Time   1 to 2 minutes

Optimal Number of Participants   From two to as many as are in the training

How to Conduct the Activity

- Instruct participants to choose a convenient partner from the people in their immediate vicinity or by any creative selection method your allotted time allows.
- Explain the rules by reminding participants of what a "high" and "low" five are all about. If you have international or multigenerational learners, you may have to provide a more detailed explanation.
- Then, ask the pairs of partners to stand back to back.
- Tell the participants that they will be doing "low fives" from this position using both their right and left arms and that the point of the game is to see how many "low fives" each pair of partners can do in 30 seconds.
- When you're sure everyone understands the rules, run one or two practice rounds. Then call for a "real" round of the game.
- Say "start" or "go," and begin your timing device.
- Randomly ask how many "low fives" each pair of partners was able to do and declare the pair with the most to be the winner.
- You can repeat the activity if you have time.

8   Nose/Ear Switch

Description   This activity requires that the participants grab their noses and ears according to your instructions. Your participants will find it hard to look graceful or coordinated while doing this activity even if they have good hand/eye coordination.

Materials Needed   No special materials needed

Time   1 to 2 minutes

Optimal Number of Participants   1 or more

How to Conduct the Activity

- *Note*—this activity might require some at home practice on your own so that you can demonstrate it for your learners.
- Ask the participants to stand up and face you.
- Tell them that this activity involves grabbing their noses and ears with their hands and that you will provide instructions. Say that the activity might sound easy, but warn them that this is not the case.
- Next, demonstrate the activity by grabbing your own nose with your left hand, then crossing over and grabbing your left ear with your right hand. You then switch the order, so that your right hand goes to your nose and your left hand crosses over and grabs your right ear. Do this several times to show it can be done.
- Now, ask the participants to follow your lead. Ask them to grab their own noses with their left hands and then cross over and grab their left ears with their right hands. Then, ask them to reverse the order, so that their right hands grab their noses and their left hands cross over and grab their right ears. Repeat this several times slowly so that the participants can practice, and then ask them if they're ready to play the game.

- Tell participants that when you say "go," they are to grab their noses with their left hands and their ears with their right hands. Then, when you say "switch," they are to switch the "grab" with right hands grabbing their noses and left hands grabbing their ears.

- Say that you will slowly decrease the time between hand switches to see who can keep up.

- You can use this activity multiple times and take breaks between nose/ear switch segments.

9   Stand Up When You Know

Description   This activity is good for a brain break in the middle of intensive content review. Instead of asking participants to hold up their hands when they respond to a question, ask them to stand up and give the answer.

Materials Needed   Prepared questions and answers to your content review

Time   5 to 10 minutes

Optimal Number of Participants   6 or more

How to Conduct the Activity

- Explain that the exercise will give participants a break from content review because they'll have to stand up to answer questions. Explain what type of questions you'll be asking, and say that only answers delivered standing up will be accepted.
- Tell the participants that they may consult with other participants or use notes or the Internet (smart phones), if available, to answer the questions. Say that those answering the questions correctly should continue to stand as each round proceeds and others work to join them
- Pose the first content review question (or brain-break question) and remind the participants again of the need to stand up to give the answer
- Continuing asking questions until all the participants are standing.
- You can continue with a standing content review session (or brain break) or end the activity. Either way this activity is an assessment tool that produces a quick "state" change for your learners.

10   Content Switch

Description   Use this very simple brain break to help learners shift their brain's focus to a new content area. As simplistic as it sounds, just changing seats is enough of an environmental change to spur episodic learning (learning associated with a mental picture of the location where an event or learning occurred).

Materials Needed   No special materials needed

Time   3 to 4 minutes

Optimal Number of Participants   4 or more

How to Conduct the Activity

- Preface this activity by telling participants that "the brain is always creating a learning address for where it learns something." Say that there is cognitive advantage to learning specific content in a specific area or in a specific seat and that switching to a new area or seat when engaging new material or content helps the learning process.

- If you want to try this learning technique, it's a good idea to warn participants at the beginning of class to not settle in a particular seat because part of the training involves changing seats.

- At the end of a topic area or other change in content, tell the participants to change seats. Plan ahead how you might accomplish this so that the move is not disruptive or chaotic. Depending on the facility's seating and ease of movement, you might ask everyone to stand up and then request that the last row switch places with the first row (or any other row). You can also ask the participants to move away from their seats and return to any seat they wish.

- In any case, allow at least 60 to 90 seconds for the participants to find a new seat and get settled into their new environment.
- It's important to note that this simple exercise enhances learning not only by enhancing episodic memory, but that all movement and environmental change produces a better learning state for the participants.

11   Simple Exercise

Description   Of course, one of the most obvious ways to give your learners a brain break is to take an "exercise" break. This can include stretching, walking in place, cross-lateral movements (such as touching the opposite knee, foot, or thigh in a continuous fashion, touching hands to the opposite foot), or even simple yoga movements if you happen to have this expertise.

Materials Needed   No special materials needed

Time   1 to 5 minutes

Optimal Number of Participants   1 or more

How to Conduct the Activity

- Clearly, not every training facility will accommodate jumping jacks and arm-waving activities, but even walking in place and simple stretching exercises while standing in place are enough to provide a brain break.
- If the space and time in your schedule is available, then doing a more energetic exercise regime inside or outside the training facility can have significant brain-break benefit, including boosting the participants' state.
- Finally, these breaks don't have to be strictly organized (especially if participants have room to fully move their bodies). Give participants a range of activities, such as light stretching, walking in place, upper body jumping jacks (waving your arms), bending over, and touching knees (i.e., left hand, right knee; right knee, left hand), and so on. Use your imagination and have fun while increasing content retention.

12   Discussion Movement

Description   Sometimes a content area lends itself to discussion. For example, the content might be focused on the advantages and disadvantages of different leadership, management, or communication styles. You can take advantage of brain preferences for learning, including episodic and state change principles, using these techniques.

Materials Needed   No special materials needed

Time   5 to 10 minutes

Optimal Number of Participants   8 or more

How to Conduct the Activity

- Imagine that the training content is focused on the benefits of social media versus traditional marketing techniques. Instead of simply asking participants for their random views while they remain in their seats, create two-to-four discussion areas (left and right sides of the room or even the four corners if your wish) and ask or assign participants to join a discussion side (point of view).
- Just the movement alone will have brain-break benefit, but the learner's environmental change switches on the benefits of episodic memory.
- How you conduct the discussion groups is up to you, so follow models you're comfortable using, including such familiar ones as group discussion followed by a report out from a chosen group member. You can even capture the output for later discussion in class.
- Remember the point of the activity is movement and the use of brain breaks to create a more effective learning environment.

13   Improvisational Throw

Description   If your learners are particularly creative and perhaps uninhibited, this brain break is particularly appropriate since it involves throwing and catching imaginary objects tossed from one learner to the next. This exercise has particularly good potential as a brain break due to the "acting" involved.

Materials Needed   No special materials needed

Time   5 to 8 minutes

Optimal Number of Participants   8 or more

How to Conduct the Activity

- Ask the participants to stand up and prepare to toss objects of their choosing (albeit imaginary ones) to other learners. If space is available, this activity works particularly well if participants are gathered in a circle.
- Explain that the imaginary objects can be anything, but the person throwing the object, which they should identify, and the recipient must be convincing in their roles. For example, they should improvise appropriate grimacing and groaning for heavy objects.
- Give examples if you wish, such as a baseball, basketball, brick, or even something disgusting that they might not want to throw or catch like a soiled diaper. Note to the participants that no matter the object, the participants watching should "feel" the weight of the thrown brick or the recoil from catching a baseball thrown at full speed.
- You should continue the game until everyone has gotten a chance to either throw or catch an object.

14   Silent Introductions

Description   Participants take a creative brain break in this exercise by pretending they cannot speak and must introduce themselves and communicate something about themselves with only body movements. Note the potential for increasing blood flow though the pantomime required for this activity.

Materials Needed   No special materials needed

Time   3 to 5 minutes

Optimal Number of Participants   4 or more

How to Conduct the Activity

- Ask your participants to pick a partner for this brain-break exercise. You can use any effective and/or creative partner selection method you wish, including random choice or previous partners from other exercises.
- Say that each of the partners will have an opportunity to convey some basic fact, describe some strong interest, or communicate some likes or dislikes to their partner using body movement and expressions alone. For example, if someone likes golf, the participant might pretend to be setting a ball up on a tee and then swinging through the imaginary ball.
- Let the participants pantomime through a few cycles of this activity before ending it.
- Like the previous Improvisational Throw activity, this exercise offers an excellent brain break since it too involves movement and "acting."

15   Vacation Writing

Description   This brain break requires learners to describe their dream vacation using body movements alone. The activity involves a lot of movement and is particularly appropriate for a group of uninhibited learners, but even less outgoing learners soon get in the spirit.

Materials Needed   No special materials needed

Time   2 to 3 minutes

Optimal Number of Participants   1 is okay, but 4 or more would be better

How to Conduct the Activity

- Ask trainees to stand at their seats and explain the activity.
- Tell them that you'll be asking questions about their dream vacation that they must answer with body motion alone, using their heads, elbows, and hips as pens to "write out" answers, along with any clarifying body movements.
- Once you're sure they understand the directions, begin the activity by asking these questions or any other questions about a dream vacation:
  ○ What is your favorite vacation spot? Write it in the air using just your head.
  ○ What is your favorite vacation drink? Write it in the air using only your left elbow.
  ○ What's your favorite food on this dream vacation? Write it in the air using only your right elbow.
  ○ What's your favorite activity on your dream vacation? Write it in the air using only your right hip.

○ What's the best tourist spot on your vacation? Write it in the air using only your left hip.

■ Some may be reluctant to do this activity at first, but once a few start answering the questions nearly all will participate and have some brain-break fun.

16   Please Stand Up

Description   This brain break allows for standing while participants answering simple "yes" or "no" questions about themselves.

Materials Needed   Prepare a list of questions, some of which will elicit a "yes" response from participants. This is a very quick activity that is an alternative to simply asking your learners to stand up and stretch for their brain break.

Time   1 to 2 minutes

Optimal Number of Participants   4 or more

How to Conduct the Activity

- Prepare 10 to 20 simple declarative questions, such as "Do you have brown hair?") for your class. If you think you can "wing" it, that's okay as well.
- Tell the participants that you are going to ask them a series of questions. If their answer is "yes," they should stand up for just a few seconds and then sit back down
- Here are some sample questions to begin with:
  - Are you a baseball fan?
  - Have you been in the same job for longer than 10 years?
  - Do you wear glasses?

17   Stand and Breathe

Description   Most of us think that there's nothing special about breathing (that is, it just happens), but full deep breathing is the first doorway to relaxation—and in our case, to a brain break.

Materials Needed   No special materials needed

Time   3 to 5 minutes

Optimal Number of Participants   Individual activity

How to Conduct the Activity

- Since many trainers do use breathing breaks, a lot of explanation is not needed. However, if you haven't done it already, do a little research about the effects of breathing to share with your learners. For example, you might tell participants before beginning the activity that breath and breathing affects with our bodies, emotions, and peace of mind, and that when our breath is calm, all three of these are also a peaceful state.
- Ask the participants to stand, close their eyes, and focus on their breath and breathing.
- Tell them to relax and try to breathe slowly and deeply. Give them a few moments to relax.
- Then lead them in focused breathing as follows:
  - ○ Ask participants to breathe slowing through their noses for three counts and then hold that breath for three counts.
  - ○ Then, tell them to release the breath slowly through their mouths.
  - ○ Continue following this round of breathing for a period of four to five minutes then end the activity.
- It's surprising how effective this simple breathing brain break can be!

18   Stand and Squeeze

Description   This brain break combines the relaxation benefits of breathing and a technique for progressive muscle relaxation that provides a surprisingly effective brain break and is also a great stress reducer.

Materials Needed   No special materials needed

Time   3 to 5 minutes

Optimal Number of Participants   Individual activity

How to Conduct the Activity

- Ask the participants to stand and allow their hands to hang loosely at their sides (i.e., not in their pockets or any other habitual way).
- Tell them that this activity will reduce stress and allow them to be more focused on the content.
- Next, ask them to make a fist with each hand and squeeze each fist firmly for a count of three (you provide the count). Repeat this exercise five to six times.
- Now, lead the participants through the stand and breath activity described in brain break 17.
- Finally, combine the breathing and fist clenching activities.
- Tell the participants to close their eyes and match the tightening of their fists to the slow intake of air used in focused breathing.
- Then, on the third count, ask them to slowly breathe out and match their slow exhale with the slow loosening of their fists. It's a real dual purpose activity.

SUMMARY

Movement and brain breaks should be a part of every presentation or learning activity that lasts more than 30 minutes. You need to give careful thought to the appropriateness of these activities for your particular audience, the length of the session, and the type of content. Remember that if your participants haven't stood up in 30 minutes, you are absolutely at risk of losing their attention, enthusiasm, and motivation to learn. Even more critically, they will lose their ability to recall and use what they've learned back on the job for better performance and return on investment.

KEY CONCEPTS

- Brain breaks are a critical part of any training facilitation.
- Brain breaks are short (1- to 2-minute) bursts of movement that change state and refresh the brain and body.
- Brain breaks enhance training by:
  - Reducing sitting time.
  - Creating more circulation of blood flow around the brain and body.
  - Providing a break and refocusing learners.
  - Creating motivation.
  - Improving the learning state.
  - Engaging the senses.
  - Reducing stress.

18 BRAIN-BREAK PRINCIPLES WORKSHEET

This chapter discussed 18 activities to encourage brain breaks. Review each of the activities discussed and jot down how you are currently using or planning to use these principles in your future learning events.

Brain-Break Activities	Currently Use	Plan to Use	How will you incorporate these brain-break activities into current and future training programs?
Time for a Partner Participants partner with each other using an 8-, 10-, or 12-segment "clock" that encourages connection with other participants.			
Famous Quotes This is an alternative activity to Clock Partners that uses quotes as a way to partner versus time for a partner.			
Walk 'n' Talk Participants partner and go for a walk together to provide time and movement to discuss training-related content.			
1-2-3 Math! A variation on rock, paper, scissors to solve simple math equations.			
Finger Snatch Partners try to grab the finger of their partner while simultaneously trying to prevent their partner from grabbing their own finger.			
Handshake Fact Participants review material each time they find one of five different partners with whom to shake hands.			

Brain-Break Activities	Currently Use	Plan to Use	How will you incorporate these brain-break activities into current and future training programs?
Back-to-Back Low Five While standing back to back, partners swing to the same side at the same time and give each other low fives as quickly as possible.			
Nose/Ear Switch While grabbing their noses and crossing over to the opposite ear with the other hand, participants are asked to switch hand positions.			
Stand Up When You Know Instead of the standard practice of raising one's hand to answer a question, participants are asked to stand up when they know an answer.			
Content Switch Whenever there is a significant change in material or content, participants are asked to change seats. Good for episodic or environmental memory.			
Simple Exercise This is a simple exercise break through the use of any number of activities, including walking in place, stretching, and doing cross-laterals, light yoga and the like.			
Discussion Movement When learning dictates group discussion, this activity moves participants to specific areas in the room where they stand and discuss.			

(continues)

Brain-Break Activities	Currently Use	Plan to Use	How will you incorporate these brain-break activities into current and future training programs?
Improvisational Throw Participants circle up and toss imaginary objects to one another, throwing and receiving as if they are real.			
Silent Introductions Participants are asked to introduce themselves to each other through descriptive movements only—no talking.			
Vacation Writing Participants use different parts of their bodies to "air" write the answers to specific questions about their favorite vacations.			
Please Stand Up This is an alternative to simply asking your learners to stand up and stretch for their brain break.			
Stand and Breathe Full deep breathing is the first doorway to relaxation—and in our case to a brain break.			
Stand and Squeeze A surprisingly effective brain break that combines the relaxation benefits of breathing and a technique for progressive muscle relaxation.			

Note

1. Daniela Schmid, Ph.D., epidemiologist, Department of Epidemiology and Preventive Medicine, University of Regensburg, Regensburg, Germany; Graham Colditz, M.D., DrPH, associate director, Prevention and Control, Siteman Cancer Center, Washington University, St. Louis, Mo.; June 16, 2014, *Journal of the National Cancer Institute, 106(7)*): dju206 (2014) doi: 10.1093/jnci/dju206.

CHAPTER 5

Team-Building Activities

Team-building activities break down communication barriers and facilitate the building of essential trust bonds among training participants. Moreover, team-building activities help all learners play to their strengths. At the same time, team-building activities—especially movement-based ones—create commonly shared metaphors that build relationships and encourage the achievement of organizational goals.

This chapter offers 10 different movement-based team-building activities that you can adjust to meet the needs of a particular training event. As a trainer focused on creating an effective learning environment, I try to include a team-building activity in as many of my training designs as possible. Not all trainers share this approach. Some view this community and relationship building experience as peripheral to the learning experience unless the training is specifically focused on building or enhancing team behaviors. However, from a brain-based perspective, the emotional connections built by even the simplest team-building activity pays considerable productivity dividends when participants return to their jobs and begin to apply what they've learned.

> *No matter what accomplishments you make, somebody helped you.*
> Althea Gibson, professional tennis player

One note of advice when you use the activities offered in this chapter or any other team-building activity is to make sure that your participants understand the purpose and goal behind their participation. Otherwise, it's easy for learners to dismiss these activities as useless and perhaps even patronizing.

EMOTIONAL CONNECTIONS AND LONG-TERM MEMORY

So, why do I believe that team-building activities enhance training retention? Like many convictions we hold, mine is based on research and experience. On the research side, Zins, Bloodworth, Weissberg, and Walberg (2007) reported that there is a definite link between a learner's social connection and emotional health to learning success.[1] Markos and Sridevi (2010) investigated the importance of emotional connection to success in the workplace and stated emphatically that "engaged employees are emotionally attached to their organization and highly involved in their job with great enthusiasm."[2]

My experience tells me that the more connection I build among individual training participants, the greater the content recall and eventual application on the job. Moreover, team-building activities enhance the learning experience by creating a positive learning environment that is strengthened through risk taking, cooperative learning, and peer teaching.

And, the bottom line for training professionals is that a positive emotional environment helps you succeed and demonstrate your value, because the emotional environment is critical to the success of the training that builds your worth to the organization.

10 TEAM-BUILDING ACTIVITIES

The 10 team- or relationship-building activities that follow are designed for easy execution and don't require a great deal of advanced work. The suggestions are meant to be open ended and adaptable to your preferences and individual training situations. However, all do share the common goal of creating team and organizational bonding.

1   Ankle Walk

Description   This activity is intended to serve as a metaphor for not only creating goals but also encouraging the follow-through that is often missing with any goal we set. Note that I've devoted extra time to this activity because of the issue's importance in all organizations.

Materials Needed

- Pen and paper for recorder
- Distribution of the P.L.A.N. via a worksheet or PowerPoint slide
- Goal-setting worksheet

Time   Ankle Walk: 8 to 10 minutes; Full Goal-Setting Activity: 1 hour

Optimal Number of Participants   At least 1 group of 5 or 6

How to Conduct the Activity

- Ask (or assign as you wish) participants to create groups of 5 or 6 participants. *Note:* Since this activity does require space to move around, make sure the training space will accommodate the activity before designing it into the learning.
- Once the groups are formed, ask each group to appoint a recorder for the activity and make sure that person has a pen and paper to do the job.
- Tell the participants—with the exception of the recorder—to form a line side by side, with everyone facing in the same direction.
- Make sure that each person's foot is touching their neighbor's foot on either side down the line (this is important for the activity). Of course, the individuals on either end will not

have anyone touching their outside foot. That's okay and does not affect the activity.

- Now, give the groups their instructions. Tell the participants that the goal of each connected group is to walk 10 to 15 feet and remain connected, that is, their feet must be touching throughout the "walk"—no disconnecting. All members of the team can participate in developing strategy and assessing each plan.

- Tell the recorders to observe and record their team's efforts to perform the walk. They'll record strategy and also note how many attempts it took to fulfill the instructions. When the activity is complete, recorders will be asked to provide an overview of their team's activities.

- Explain that while some groups do get it right the first time, on subsequent tries they will likely fail, so it's important for recorders to take notes and observe to fulfill their roles.

- Once all the participants understand the directions, start the activity.

- The teams may need a number of attempts to get it right, but all will eventually figure it out and learn some key success principles though a fundamental brain-body connection.

As simple as this process seems, it is one of the fundamentals of continuing success, yet most people don't know it, use it, or follow through on the entire process. This activity allows trainees to experience these key success principals through the brain-body connection, which is a physical connection. It also sets up a simple, yet profound, goal-setting discussion based on the following pneumonic (PLAN):

Plan Your Vision
List the Actions
Assess the Outcomes
New Approach (If Necessary)

Though this chapter is about team-building through movement activities, this particular activity acts as an appropriate lead-in to a very important skill for individuals or teams. Below is the four-step success PLAN for change and achievement through goal setting. In all its simplicity, it will never fail is there is complete follow through. If you continue on past the movement activity, here are some key concepts to consider:

1. **P**lan your vision. Begin with the end goal as your starting point. In other words, you must set goals. To get where you're going, setting goals is essential because it creates positive pressure. It not only gives your brain something to focus on, but creates a sense of "I'm here and want to be there." This creates good pressure, energy, motion and action, which gives your brain a map and helps you to take action toward the attainment of a particular goal.

2. **L**ist your actions, or create an action plan. Many people set goals and even write them down, but they fail to create a plan of action that is specific and absolutely necessary for achievement. An action plan becomes a map for achievement. It lets our brains know exactly what to do to reach our goals. Creating a goal without an action plan is like piloting a flight to a new destination without a map.

3. **A**ssess the outcomes or notice whether the plan is working or not! Whatever your goal is, it's very important to be aware of whether you're moving closer to your goal or further away. If you have made it to the point of creating an action plan, it is important to continually check your progress! Most people fail on the first two steps! If they make it this far, it can be a real sticking point. Plan A sounds great, Plan B can be difficult to create, and Plan C is essential after two failed attempts. Are you willing?

4. If Plan A is not working, determine a **N**ew approach. It's scary to create goals because you might fail, but failure can be a great teacher as long as it stays a teacher and not a jailer. People who set goals are taking risks. They are putting themselves out there by telling the world or themselves they want to achieve this goal. Because of this, people often quit if their plan does not work out. This requires a change in perspective! If a plan doesn't work, let it be a teacher! Now you know what doesn't work! It's a free education. Now is the time to change your approach and, if the new approach doesn't work, change it again, and if that doesn't work, then change it again! You'll eventually get it right!

GOAL-SETTING WORKSHEET

Use this Ankle Walk debrief sheet to help your team improve their performance and meet their goals during the activity.

Step 1—PLAN Your Vision. Team members must walk 10 to 15 feet as a single unit without their touching feet losing contact. What is your vision for achieving this goal?

- _____
- _____
- _____
- _____

Step 2—LIST Your Actions. What strategies will you use to accomplish this goal?

- _____
- _____
- _____
- _____

Step 3—ASSESS the Outcomes. How well did the plan work?

- _____
- _____
- _____
- _____

Step 4—NEW Approach (if necessary). If the original plan fails, what new strategy would you develop and execute?

- _____
- _____
- _____
- _____

2   Floating Balloon

Description   This activity is intended to help team members bond through fun and possible light competition. Team members attempt to keep multiple balloons in the air while gathered in a circle holding hands.

Materials Needed

- Large balloons blown up to about volley-ball size. You will have to blow them up. I've always done this before the training begins. You will need a maximum of 4 balloons per team, so if you have 4 teams, you will need 16 balloons.
- Open space for several teams to form circles of 8 to 10 people

Time   8 to 10 minutes

Optimal Number of Participants   At least 1 group of 6; groups of 10 to 12 are optimal

How to Conduct the Activity

- Divide the participants into three or four equal teams (6 to 12 in a group).
- Then ask the team members to make a small, tight circle and join hands.
- Explain the game and rule. Tell them that their task is to keep as many balloons aloft as possible within their own circle using any part of their bodies except their hands. Tell them that if the balloon moves outside the circle, the entire connected team must move together in order to capture it.
- Once the teams understand the game, throw in a practice balloon. After a few minutes throw in another balloon. When you think the teams are ready, begin the game. One of your tasks is continue to distribute balloons to groups by throw-

ing a balloon into each group one at a time. If you have four groups, each group will be given one balloon to begin the activity. Then you will give them a second and so on (yes, you will be scrambling around the room). It has been my experience that even the most athletic of groups (for example, physical education teachers) cannot handle more than three balloons at a time without one falling to the ground. Continue the activity for a predetermined amount of time (1 to 2 minutes) each time you play once all three balloons have been distributed to each team.

- Debrief by asking what attributes of team building did this activity provide? You'll get answers such as teamwork, collaboration, communication, quick decisions, changing directions when necessary, laughter, etc.

- The game can produce a friendly competition if wanted. Simply, if a team drops a balloon they receive a point. This means achieving a score of "0" is desirable.

- The exercise and diversion is a good brain break in addition to an activity that teaches team values.

3   Learn My Name

Description   The objective is to help participants learn the names of new team members through a fast–action, ball-passing activity.

Materials Needed

- Several balls (sports balls or even balloons)
- Chairs for all participants
- A whistle

Time   8 to 10 minutes

Optimal Number of Participants   8 to 32

How to Conduct the Activity

- Ask the participants to make a small, tight circle with their chairs.
- Explain that the game will teach them the names of their team members.
- Tell them that the game begins by their passing a ball around their circle of chairs. Each person receiving the passed ball must say his or her name out loud.
- Explain that the ball will be passed one to two times around the circle. Note that they should listen carefully to the names as they are called out.
- Say that once the ball has made a few circuits around the circle, the second phase of the game begins. In this phase, the person holding the ball must say the name of the person sitting directly to their right. If the name can't be recalled, the ball remains with the holder. At some point, at your discretion, add another ball or two to the game.

    Since the goal of the game is to not be stuck holding any balls, it's advantageous to learn the names so the ball can be passed. Say that this is an important point to note, especially when multiple balls are traveling around the circle.

- Inform participants that if a whistle is sounded, the ball-passing direction switches from right to left and that any player holding two balls must leave the game.
- When the participants are ready, start the game.
- *Note*: You don't want to eliminate participants for long, so invite eliminated players back quickly and place them in a different seat. In fact, switching seating throughout the game is a good idea to ensure names are learned.

Alternative version   If you're working with a large number of participants, create two teams and play the game the same way. You can add the element of competition by counting down the participants and dividing them up by odd and even numbers. When someone is stuck with two balls or drops a ball, the game is stopped. Or, if an odd-number team member drops the ball or is stuck with two balls, the even numbered team gets a point. The opposite will be true if an even numbered person makes the mistake.

4   I Wish I Could

Description   Participants learn about the unique talents, hobbies, or experiences of other team members while building vital and productive relationships.

Materials Needed

- Name tags or large mailing labels
- Markers or pens

Time   15 to 30 minutes

Optimal Number of Participants   12 or more

How to Conduct the Activity

- Pass out name tags or index cards to participants.
- Ask them to write a talent, experience, hobby, or belief about themselves on the tag or card. Give some examples, such as "love to read," "skydiver," "actor," "happy person," and so on. Then, ask them to attach the name tag or label at their shoulder level so it's easy to read.
- Now, before asking the participants to begin mingling with their teammates, provide the introduction to this activity. Say the activity might reveal hidden dreams or talents.
- Explain that their job is to walk around the room and notice what others have identified as their skills, hobbies, or interests. If you like the fact that another team member flies airplanes on the weekend and your dream is to learn how to fly, ask to trade tags with that person.
- Tell participants they can make up to three trades during the exercise.

■ When the participants have finished trading, gather them as a group and select some participants to explain why they made the trades they did. If you have the time, let the original owner of the tag talk about his or her hobby, skill, or interest.

5   Name Tag Switch

Description   This activity enhances team bonds and builds cooperative, collegial, and community-focused relationships by asking participants to reveal some unique or important aspect of their lives to others.

Materials Needed

- Name tags or large mailing labels
- Pens or pencils

Time   15 to 30 minutes

Optimal Number of Participants   12 or more

How to Conduct the Activity

- Pass out name tags and a pen or pencil to each participant.
- Explain the activity by telling them to write a brief sentence or series of words using adjectives that describes some essential aspect of their personality or interests. Give a few examples, such as "I exercise every day," "I read every day," or "mother of three boys." Remind them NOT to write their names on the tags.
- Now collect all the completed tags and randomly redistribute them to the participants, with the instruction to stand up and mingle with each other.
- Explain that their job is to discover the true owner of the tag they are holding through conversation and deductive reasoning. Tell the participants to return the tag to its rightful owner.
- Depending on the amount of time you have, allow this discovery process to continue until a number of these connections have been made. Then ask participants to return to their seats and give the unmatched tags to their owners. You can

reunite unmatched tags in any way you wish, including asking holders of unmatched tags to read the contents out loud to the entire class.

- Once all the tags are returned, ask participants to explain a particular sentence or descriptive phase that appears on their tag.

6   Shared Unique Experiences

Description   The objective of this activity is to uncover new information about other team members through the use of a series of "unusual questions."

Materials Needed

■ A predetermined list of questions about unique experiences (example questions provide below, but feel free to create your own).

■ Depending on the room configuration and seating type and arrangement, chairs are needed for all participants.

Time   15 to 20 minutes

Optimal Number of Participants   6 or more

How to Conduct the Activity

■ Ask the participants to form a circle with their desks and/or chairs.

■ Explain that you want them to respond out loud with a "yes" or "no" as you read from a list of "have-you-ever" questions. Tell them that if they do answer "yes," they must come to the center of the room and shake the hand(s) of anyone else who answered "yes" to that particular question. Say that as part of the activity they'll be asked to share their "have-you-ever" story. Depending on time and the number of participants, you may have to choose to hear just a few stories.

■ Begin the activity by asking questions such as:
  ○ Have you ever climbed to the highest mountain in your home state?
  ○ Have you ever lived overseas for more than six months?
  ○ Have you ever performed in karaoke bar?

- ○ Have you ever been without a shower for more than one week?
- ○ Do you have more than two siblings?
- ○ Have you ever ridden an elephant?
- ○ Have you ever spoken another language exclusively (not your native language) for a year or more?
- ○ Have you ever been in love with someone who was vegetarian?
- ○ Have you ever ridden in a helicopter?
- ○ Have you ever broken four or more bones in your body?
- ○ Have you done volunteer work in the past six months?
- ○ Have you ever been rock climbing and repelled down a mountain?
- ○ Have you ever had a close relative or friend who lived 100 years or more?
- ○ Have you ever cooked a meal by yourself for more than 20 people?
- ○ Have you ever been to a Super Bowl, World Series, Olympics, or World Cup?
- ○ Have you ever been parachuting or done a bungee jump?
- ○ Have you ever seen a polar, grizzly or black bear other than in a zoo?
- ■ Note that sometimes a few participants are not able to answer "yes" to any of your questions. If this happens, you can involve those participants by inviting them to come to the center of the circle and ask the group "have-you-ever" questions based on their own unique experiences.

7   Rock, Paper, Scissors, Tag

Description   Team building happens as a consequence of this activity that is full of fun, movement, teamwork, and competition.

Materials Needed

■ Tape, such as masking or painter's tape
■ A large training space. If the training space is not large enough and no larger external space is available, you might try moving seats and/or tables out of the way.

Time   15 to 20 minutes

Optimal Number of Participants   10 to 20

How to Conduct the Activity

■ Divide the participants into two evenly numbered teams (if possible) and mark off a line in the middle of the room with tape. Each team should be on opposite sides of the tape.
■ Explain that the activity relies on the Rock, Paper, Scissors game and demonstrate just to make sure everyone knows how it's played.

Two people stand face to face. At the same time, each person pounds one of his or her own fists into the opposite hand three times while saying rock (1), paper (2), scissors (3)—"SHOOT!" On the saying of "SHOOT," each individual stops pounding their fist and shows their partner a rock (closed fist), paper (flat hand), or scissors (peace sign turned on its side). The rules are simple: paper covers rock (paper wins); rock smashes scissors (rock wins); scissors cuts paper (scissors wins). For example if one partner shoots a rock and the other partner shoots paper, the partner who shot paper wins (because of the above rules). If two partners shoot the same thing (both shoot paper), the game is replayed. Now, for playing it as a team . . .(hang on tight!)

- Explain that each team will "huddle" at a designated area when the game begins and strategize together whether to "shoot" rock, paper, or scissors for the current round of play.
- Say that once a team decides on a strategy, the entire team will form a horizontal line that is one step back from the challenge line marked by the tape.
- Tell them that when the activity begins, you will lay down the challenge, rock, paper, scissors, shoot, and all the team members will "shoot" their agreed upon symbol in unison. I have always used an "8" count steady beat. As leader, I say "1, 2, ready, go." At this point, both groups join in, saying: "rock, paper, scissors, shoot!"
- Finally, explain that the game involves an additional element of movement. The losing team must quickly turn and walk quickly to a previously designated safety zone (maybe 15 feet away from the center line). The winning team is allowed to "chase down and tag" the losing team members who are not able to make it to the safety zone Note, you can pick any appropriate area in the room for this purpose. It's important to emphasize to the participants that "chase" for this activity does not mean run; it means only that participants walk as fast as possible.
- Part of the fun of this activity is to quickly figure out which team has won and which team has lost!
- Say that any losing team member tagged must join the winner's team.
- When you're sure the participants understand the game, send them to their respective sides and begin the activity.

■ Allow a few moments for the opposing teams to discuss their strategy. Then call the teams to the challenge line and call out: "rock, paper, scissors, shoot!"

■ After the "chase" is over and new team members tagged, allow a few minutes for the teams to regroup and call for round 2. Repeat as time allows.

■ It is interesting to see how some participants react very quickly, while other students seem unsure what to do. You might use some of these observations in any team training that follows.

8   Elbow to Elbow

Description   Teams learn to think differently when approaching a task or solving a problem in this fun and quick-paced activity.

Materials Needed

- 1 ball or balloon per group

Time   5 to 8 minutes

Optimal Number of Participants   6 or more

How to Conduct the Activity

- Clear a space and ask the participants to stand in a circle. Pass out one inflated balloon or ball to one person in the circle. This will be the starting point of the activity (the balloon will be used from now on for explanatory purposes). Ask the participant to pinch the balloon between his or her elbows to demonstrate the technique for passing the balloon and then explain that the goal of the activity is to pass the balloon from one member to the next as quickly as possible using only their elbows.
- Start by saying "Go!" Participants should continue passing the balloon until it moves around the circle one time.
- Next, have participants discuss what would help them be more efficient and pass the ball more quickly. If wanted they can change places in the circle.
- Now ask groups to "reverse" and move the balloon in the opposite direction.
- Tell the participants to practice passing the balloon and then call for the start of the game.
- Note that you can increase the challenge by adding more balloons to the circle.

- If a participant drops the balloon, he or she simply picks it up using hands (or elbows, you decide) and puts it back between his or her elbows and continues passing it around.

9   Triangle Tag

Description   Use this activity if you want to add some fast-paced movement that really gets your participant's hearts pumping and blood flowing through their bodies.

Materials Needed   No special materials

Time 8 to 10 minutes

Optimal Number of Participants   1 group of 4 or more

How to Conduct the Activity

- Divide participants into groups of four.
- Explain that this activity is a variation of a "tag-you're-it" game.
- Instruct three members of each group to hold hands, closing themselves off to the fourth group member.
- Tell each group of three holding hands that they must choose one member to be their "it" player. The remaining member (the person not holding anyone's hands and standing outside the triangle) is the designated "tag" player.
- The goal is for the "tag" player to move from side to side in an effort to tag the "it" player, while the triangle members continue moving to keep the "it" player safe.
- Once the rules are understood, tell the groups to make their "it" and "tag" choices and then let them have a practice round before formally beginning the activity.
- Note that although this game can be played in a smaller training space at a slower speed, it will be more effective in a larger space. (This is a great opportunity to take your participants outside if that is an option!)
- Switch roles of team members several times.

10   The Human Touch

Description   This activity is designed to emphasize the need for delegation and shared sharing responsibility to accomplish organizational goals. This activity can also act as a quick brain break.

Materials Needed   No special materials needed

Time   3 to 5 minutes

Optimal Number of Participants   8 or more

How to Conduct the Activity

- Ask participants to stand up and find a partner.
- Once partners are selected, ask them to face each other while you give the instructions.
- Tell them to raise their hands and touch palms (or clasp fingers) as if they were standing in front of a mirror. (Note, the touching makes this activity more stable.)
- Once the participants are in position, ask them to slowly step back and notice how much more difficult it is to work together as they back away from each other.
- It's a simple activity, but it does make the point about how working closely with team members is much easier than working apart. It illustrates the importance of support and working together.

KEY CONCEPTS

- Team-building activities create essential bonds between participants that are critical for the emotional health of the team.

- Team-building activities, especially those that are movement based, create common metaphors that build relationships and encourage the achievement of shared organizational goals.

- From a brain-based perspective, the emotional connections offered by even the simplest team-building activity can pay considerable productivity dividends if your participants return to their jobs and apply what they've learned.

- Make sure that your participants understand the purpose and goal behind their participation in these activities. Otherwise, it's easy for learners to dismiss these activities as useless and even patronizing unless you do the work to connect the dots.

10 TEAM-BUILDING ACTIVITIES WORKSHEET

This chapter discussed 10 activities designed to encourage the building of relationships and community among team members. Review each of the activities discussed and jot down how you are currently using or plan to use these principles in your future learning events.

Team-Building Activities	Currently Use	Plan to Use	How will you incorporate these team-building activities into current and future training programs?
Ankle Walk This activity helps participants meet and achieve goals by encouraging follow through.			
Floating Balloon A fun team-building activity that encourages movement, laughter, and working to support one another.			
Learn My Name Allows for learning new names in a fun and fast-paced setting.			
I Wish I Could Allows participants to learn new and interesting facts about each other.			
Name Tag Switch Helps build a collegial community by discovering the identity of someone through the writing and sharing of a simple sentence.			
Shared Unique Experiences A set of unusual questions are answered in a movement-oriented setting that creates bonds among different team members.			

(continues)

Team-Building Activities	Currently Use	Plan to Use	How will you incorporate these team-building activities into current and future training programs?
Rock, Paper, Scissors, Tag A fast-paced version of an oldie but goody that will have your participants' heart rates up and changing teams on a moment-to-moment basis.			
Elbow to Elbow A circle pass game using only a ball or balloon held between participants' elbows as the passing mechanism.			
Triangle Tag A fast-paced activity that builds team protection for one participant and creates the metaphor for how important teammates can be.			
The Human Touch A simple activity that shows how important the support of a teammate can be.			

Notes

1. Zins, J.E., Bloodworth, M.R., Weissberg, R.P., & Walberg, H. (2004). The scientific base linking social and emotional learning to school success. In J.E. Zins, R.P. Weissberg, M.C. Wang, & HJ. Walberg (Eds.), *Building Academic Success on Social and Emotional Learning: What Does the Research Say?* New York: Teachers College Press.
2. Markos, S. & Sridevi, M.S. (2010). Employee Engagement: The Key to Improving Performance. *International Journal of Business & Management*, 5(12), 89–96.

CHAPTER 6

Content-Review Activities

Every learning professional uses some kind of rehearsal technique to increase the likelihood that participants will remember and use what they've learned in class. Sometimes rehearsal takes the form of direct point by point content review listed on a PowerPoint slide or it could be a simple question-and-answer session at the end of training.

> *For the things we have to learn before we can do them, we learn by doing them.*
>
> Aristotle, Greek philosopher

But simply reviewing content, whether displayed on PowerPoint slides or through questioning techniques, is not the most efficient way to help learners improve corporate and individual performance by retrieving and actually applying what they learn. What simple content review is missing—at least based on my experience—is a balanced approach to using movement to engage the brain's higher order thinking skills and, importantly, to make an emotional or sensory connection to the content.

Rehearsal Defined by researchers as the repetitive act of processing information. It is a key process that allows our brains to transfer content from working memory to long-term storage.[1]

This chapter offers a solid toolbox of movement activities, ranging from those that are simple and quick to implement to those requiring more trainer-directed instruction and participant engagement. Note that these suggested activities come with the caveat to use your professional judgment about when and how to use them. After all, it is not possible or advisable to use movement-based activities to help learners recall every type of content. Some content, such as the multiplication tables, may be best imprinted on our brain by repeated exposure and practice. Still, as you use the techniques that follow, you'll adapt and enhance them to fit many circumstances and situations.

FIVE CONTENT-REVIEW ACTIVITIES

The following five activities contain one partner activity, three small-group activities and one whole-group activity. Some might require alteration to fit your available training space and time. As always, you should adjust any suggested activity to fit individual circumstances.

1   Take and Talk

Description   Participants engage in a competition to "take" an object placed between them. The winner of the "take" must answer a content-review question. If the correct answer is given, the winning player receives points for the round. This game is not only fun, but it allows participants to review critical content in a way that encourages their brains to permanently store the information.

Materials Required

- Whistle or other sound-making device.
- An object(s) for participants to "take" (e.g. toy, ball, beanbag).
- Pen or pencil and paper for each participant.

Time   10 to 20 minutes

Optimal Number of Participants   Four or more, organized in pairs

How to Conduct the Activity

This activity works best if the competitors sit across from each other at a table or across another flat surface.

- Explain that the game's purpose is to review content in a fun and competitive manner and that participants will engage with each other during the activity.
- Then, arrange chairs and/or desks and tables so that the participants are sitting across from each other. It doesn't matter how the competitors are arranged. It's a level playing field for all since it's about content review of material everyone must learn.
- Once the participants are in position, place the "take" object between the players and remind them that the point of the

game is to acquire points by answering a series of questions based on the training content. Pass out pens and paper to players so they can record the correct answer after each round of play.

- Tell the participants that you will read a question and then blow a whistle (or any other game starting sound you want to use).

- Say that the first person in each pair of competitors to grab the object and answer the question correctly (the "talk" part) will receive two points.

- Point out that a player who answers incorrectly must pass the "taken" object to his or her opponent. If the opponent answers the question correctly, that person receives one point. If neither player answers correctly, no points are awarded.

- Finally, remind the participants that they must answer the question once they've captured the "take" object out loud to their partners.

- When you're sure the participants understand the game, either start the first round or, if you wish, run a test round and then start the game.

- Continue for 8 to 10 rounds, or more if wanted.

- After each round, tell the participants to write the correct answer on the sheet you provided for later review.

2 Review at "The Improv"

Description   This activity uses role-play in an unusual way—to review content. Participants form teams and collaborate to create a role play that demonstrates key content from their training session. For example, if the training content is time management, an effective role-play would be a comparison between a stressed-out individual who employs poor habits regarding time management versus a happy and organized person who makes use of the time management training suggestions that have been reviewed. The same type of comparison role-play could be used for presentation skill.

Not only does the content role-play engage the learner, but the movement charges up the brain's information processing and storage capabilities. In a corporate training setting, role-play has many uses, including sales training, and is a useful activity for making comparisons. In addition, participants get valuable practice with their presentation skills. It's a good idea to choose the content-related topics for this activity prior to beginning the class.

Materials Required   No special materials required.

Time   10 to 15 minutes

Optimal Number of Participants   At least 2 groups of 4 to 6

How to Conduct the Activity

- Divide the participants into four or five teams as appropriate for the group.
- Explain that this role-play activity will help them remember the content presented in class. Say that they must collaborate to create a movement-based role-play that "acts out" a

content topic that you will give each group. Note that there are no points in this game (although you can add this feature if you wish) and that they should try to be as creative as possible.

■ If you wish, prepare a simple example of movement-based, content-review role-play and act it out to demonstrate the concept. Otherwise, give each group at least three content concepts or other appropriate information they must communicate to the other participants through role-play and then start the activity.

■ Repeat this for as many rounds as you wish depending on time and the enthusiasm of the learners.

3   Group Webbing on the Move

Description   Webbing simply refers to a visual tool (think chart paper and markers) that organizes information in a useful way to the learner. You can think of this activity as a variation of information mind-mapping, except that instead of working alone or as a single group, all the participants share their ideas as individual teams and as a class. The other differences are the addition of movement and the requirement for silence.

Materials Required

- Large sheets of paper, such as poster board.
- Masking or painter's tape.
- Markers for each participant. You can provide different colored markers for each team to introduce more creativity into the activity.

Time   30 to 60 minutes

Optimal Number of Participants   Groups of four-to-six members works best. If groups are larger, it becomes difficult to manage the information.

How to Conduct the Activity

- Divide participants into groups. If possible, each group should have an even number of participants.
- Pass out an appropriate number of markers for each team along with poster paper or other paper choice.
- Explain the activity to the participants. Tell them that each team will pick a content topic based on the training and then write that topic choice in the center of the paper provided.
- Give a content example to make sure they understand the concept. For example, if the training was about leadership

competencies, then a topic example might be the importance of self-awareness.

■ Depending on the room configuration, participants may tape the poster paper to the wall with team members gathered around or they can work on an available table top or even the floor.

■ Remind participants that the activity is to be done silently once all the teams have chosen a topic.

■ Finally, explain how the participants will move from one team's work to the next. Say that you'll give the initially formed teams enough time to capture their ideas and comments, but then you'll call for each team to leave their work behind and move to another poster.

■ Tell them that once they arrive at the new poster, they must read the contents before adding their own ideas and questions. When team members have exhausted all the comments or questions they can add to a new poster, they must move to another one and repeat the process.

■ This activity combines movement and new viewpoints on a topic and enhances learning and recall. Note that this activity won't be totally silent since you might be fielding a few questions from participants or even suggesting a line of thinking based on the work of the participants as it progresses.

4   The "Moving" Venn Diagram

Description   Participants in this activity will need to use a Venn diagram, which uses circles to represent sets, with the position and overlap of the circles indicating the relationships between the sets. Participants read out loud the training topic content cards you provide and decide on which side of a Venn diagram to place their content. Hula-hoops are then used to create the Venn diagrams, and participants must jump into the appropriate side after reading their content cards. Once the participant makes a choice, the other group members discuss whether the correct choice was made. This is a good activity for content, including decision making and marketing, where a comparison is important to the learning. For example, salespeople may be trained about the differences between interior and exterior wayfinding, which includes signs, maps, and other graphic or audible methods for conveying location and giving direction to travelers. If the training involves a sign company, salespeople would label one side of the Venn diagram "interior" and the other side "exterior." Each team member would be given a labeled card, such "vehicular traffic," "change of seasons," or "pedestrian traffic only," and then have to place the card on the side of their choosing.

Materials Required

- Eight hula-hoops.
- 4 × 5-inch note cards or index cards with training content topics written on each. You should create enough content cards so that each participant has at least five or six to use in the activity.

Time   15 to 20 minutes

Optimal Number of Participants   Small groups of 4 to 8 members, although it could be done as one large group activity.

How to Conduct the Activity

- Divide the participants into four even groups and place two overlapping hula-hoops in each corner of the room.
- Make sure that each side of each hula-hoop and crossover section are distinctly marked so that participants have a clear choice when choosing where their particular content cards should land. For instance, in the example above, "interior," "exterior," and "both."
- Send each group to one corner of the room and give each team member a stack of content cards that you've prepared for the class.
- Explain that the cards contain topics based on class content and that this a comparison activity as suggested by the hula-hoop Venn diagrams you've placed in each corner of the room.
- Select one of the four groups to demonstrate the concept.
- Ask a participant to read the content card and then jump into the appropriate side of the hula-hoop Venn diagram.
- Tell them that once a choice has been made, the other group members must discuss the choice as it relates to the content of the training.
- Say that once the discussion ends on a particular choice, another group member must read one of the cards and repeat the discussion process.
- Tell them that this activity will continue until all the content cards are read and discussed.
- When you're sure the participants understand the directions, start the activity.

5 The Trade Review

Description Participants form a circle of chairs or desks and must get up from their seats to trade question cards as they work individually to answer them. The goal is to answer as many questions as possible in the allotted time.

Materials Required

- Worksheet with 20 square blocks marked off and numbered; one worksheet per participant (see Figure 6.1).
- Index cards with review questions written on them. Each card should include a number from 1 through 20 that corresponds to the worksheet's 20 squares.
- Pens or pencils for all participants.

Time 15 to 20 minutes

Optimal Number of Participants A maximum of 20 participants for each circle of chairs although this activity can be conducted with several groups by creating more circles to conduct the activity. You would not want to do this activity with less than 8 people.

How to Conduct the Activity

- Ask the participants to form a circle with their chairs or desks.
- Hand out the worksheet you prepared (see Figure 6.1) and explain that they will record their answers in the square blocks.
- Next, hand out one of the index cards you've prepared with a content question written on one side. Make sure you hand out the card so that participants cannot see the question and remind them they are not to turn the card over until the activity begins.

1	2	3	4	5
6	7	8	9	10
11	12	13	14	15
16	17	18	19	20

Figure 6.1 Trade Review Handout

- Tell them that each card has a number at the top that corresponds to a number on the worksheet. Say that once the activity begins, they must place the answer to the question in the appropriately numbered block on the grid.

- Inform them that after answering the initial question, each participant moves to the center of the circle to find a new question to answer. It does not matter if the question was answered correctly. In fact, they won't know until the end of the activity anyway.

- Tell them that they must move to the center of the circle and exchange cards with another participant if they don't know the answer to the initial question.

- Remind the participants again that they may not look at the questions until they return to their seats and that if the question they got during an exchange is something they've already answered, then they must get up and find another card.

- Once all participants have their answer sheets and cards, begin the activity.

- The goal is to answer as many questions as possible before the end of the activity, so the timeframe is largely up to the trainer. Note that this activity is usually done in silence, but can be adapted to your own preferences.

KEY CONCEPTS

- ■ Content review is critical to memory formation and is part of the practice and rehearsal necessary for transitioning working memory to long-term storage.

- ■ Using movement during review provides a natural brain break and involves the whole body in the review process, making it active and more in line with how the brain prefers to learn.

- ■ Reviewing content in some manner should happen on a consistent basis.

- ■ This chapter contains five content-review activities divided into partner, small-group, and whole-group activities.

- ■ Some activities may need to be adapted to meet your specific needs.

CONTENT-REVIEW ACTIVITIES WORKSHEET

This chapter discussed five activities designed to enable successful content review. Think about each of the activities discussed and jot down how you are currently using or plan to use these principles in your future learning events.

Content-Review Activities	Currently Use	Plan to Use	How will you incorporate these content-review activities into current and future training programs?
Take and Talk The winner of the "grab" must answer a content-review question in this activity. If the correct answer is given, the winning player receives points for the round.			
Review at "The Improv" Group members review concepts in a role-play setting by acting out of concepts.			
Group Webbing on the Move Team members comment and question content listed in a web format on poster paper. They then move on to all assigned posters around the room to continue to comment and question each other's work.			
The "Moving" Venn Diagram Review Groups are given content cards and instructed to place them in the appropriate sides of a Venn diagram created with hula-hoops.			
The Trade Review Participants are asked to answer questions and then move to the center of the group circle to trade questions with another group member.			

The Big Picture

- Chapter 7—The Kinesthetic Presenter
- Chapter 8—Why Movement Is a Powerful Learning Tool

Section 3 highlights three "big-picture" benefits that come from incorporating movement into your training programs. First, benefits that accrue to the learning professional, including improved presentation and facilitation skills. Second, the benefits movement gives to organizational training programs. And, third, the benefits for organizational improvement and higher performance.

CHAPTER 7

The Kinesthetic Presenter

Being an effective trainer means being an effective presenter. An important part of that discussion is exactly the point of this book—the body in motion. I would be remiss in making the case for movement in training if there were no discussion from the trainer's perspective. At its core, the body will never betray the brain. How well one is prepared, how well one is practiced, and how well the presenter's skill state is honed is almost always obvious by simply observing the body. Therefore, training can be a success or failure based on your kinesthetic awareness, your ability to sense and detect bodily position, weight, or movement of the muscles, tendons, and joints.

The human brain is programmed to learn through the movement of objects and of people and their body movements. Unfortunately, many presenters and learning professionals are reluctant to engage with this primal tendency toward movement. Instead, they drown their audiences with dozens of PowerPoint slides as a poor substitute for a true connection.

> *Suit the action to the word, the word to the action.*
>
> Shakespeare, *Hamlet*

That's a shame because body language, as most learning professionals know, is responsible for approximately 55 percent of communication between humans, with tone of voice accounting for 38 percent of the meaning. In comparison, words only communicate 7 percent of the meaning,[1] Although these numbers are not 100 percent accurate all the time, as they are based on context and emotion, they bring into focus the critical nature of body language, which includes posture, gestures, and facial messages. The critical question for all speakers, presenters, trainers, teachers, and facilitators to ask is "Do your body movements support the words, message, and emotions you are trying to convey?" When our body language doesn't agree with the tone of voice and the message we're trying to send, it creates mixed messages.

HOW WE LEARN THROUGH MOVEMENT IN OTHERS

It's probably safe to say that every learning professional understands how their success is directly tied to appropriate body language in terms of projecting authority, confidence, and engagement. But equally important is the kinesthetic message of movement, such as hand gestures and pacing. Successful presenters offer the full package to their audience so their message is communicated with passion and confidence as expressed by their voice, posture, demeanor and movements.

My personal style of presentation incorporates these research findings. I use physical movements as much as my voice to convey meaning and emotion and to connect an audience to content. You might think of this style of presentation as a choreographed dance, one in which the presenter moves freely about the room using body movements—hands, legs, feet, and posture—in concert with his or her voice to dramatically illustrate the importance of the content.

Of course, what I am describing is much more subtle than Michael Jackson floating across the room, but the effect and the emotional connection made with the audience certainly should be that effectively choreographed. Yes, it is possible for certain speakers to stand behind a podium and inspire an audience, but those people are usually presidents, kings, and perhaps a few professional motivational speakers, but even they're trained to be conscious of their body language if they're standing still. So, unless you count yourself among this group, the admonition to "move and learn" is for you, the trainer or learning professional who wants the message heard and acted on in a way the creates value for your organization.

THREE KEY RULES FOR PRESENTATIONS

- Avoid handheld microphones.
- Move as much as possible.
- Don't make your audience sit more than 30 minutes without movement.

SENSORY EXPERIENCE AND NONVERBAL MESSAGES

Researchers have long known that the brain stores information through sensory cues and that creating a full sensory experience heightens the chances that audience members will hear, understand, and implement the message they hear. We've all seen great speakers take advantage of this connection when they use practiced nonverbal messages that support their verbal messages. So how important can these nonverbal messages be to our success in life?

Recent research at Harvard and Columbia Business Schools indicates that when someone holds his or her body in an expansive, "high-power" pose (for example, if you stand tall with your legs apart and arms stretched wide or if you lean back in your chair and put your feet on the desk) for just two minutes, the result is that you will feel more powerful and confident. Moreover, this feeling is matched by hormonal changes in your body. The message is clear. Posture and body language do make a cognitive difference![2]

The rest of this chapter will show you how to actively use kinesthetic activity to connect emotionally with participants and encourage content retention.

THREE KEY KINESTHETIC PRESENTATION TECHNIQUES

Kinesthetic presentations share three main elements: movement that engages the brain, physical gestures that invite the audience to connect and participate, and an empathetic interplay between the audience and the presenter.

1. **Movement Engages the Brain.** Move about and within an audience rather than just back and forth across the board room, podium or stage. Great speakers vary the distance between themselves and the audience and make use of all available and comfortable space. Of course, sometimes a presentation is more speaker-centric (for example, motivational speaking) but you can achieve this same emotional connection by making direct eye contact with a few chosen audience members

throughout the presentation. Such intimacy of connection can be a powerful tool especially in smaller auditoriums.

2. **Use Inviting Physical Gestures.** Make sure your words and physical gestures are in synch. For example, a heartfelt sentiment about the power of organizational community building delivered while looking away from the audience with hands firmly buried in your pockets certainly won't help "sell" the message. Gestures including open arms and hands, walking toward someone or a group of individuals, and bringing your outreached hand to a closed fist against your chest says "we." That's why it's important to think about and even rehearse appropriate movement—body language and posture, hand gestures, facial expressions—as part of any presentation preparation routine. Remember that preparation is the cornerstone of comfort. So, don't forgo direct practice, first alone in front of a mirror and then with every audience to build your competence at connecting emotionally with your audience through physical movement and the verbal queues you provide.

> *The tone of the presentation is set before the presentation begins.*
>
> Timothy Koegel, author of *The Exceptional Presenter*

3. **Remain Aware of Your Audience.** Finally, great kinesthetic-minded speakers are keenly aware of their audience's state— the physical needs of their audience, that is, if "energy" or attention is waning because of hunger, room temperature, or other factors—and actively take steps to manage it. For example, simply modulating your voice, speaking from different locations in a room, and moving when making a point

will satisfy our brain's need for novelty and reengage the listener. Of course, as we've discussed in this book, physically engaging audiences in an activity is a direct intervention, but this strategy is not always available. Still, even small changes can make all the difference in an audience's level of engagement.

CREATING AN IMPRESSION

Passion and emotion are the most powerful training tools, but your body's movements can quickly undermine your message. Remember, you have 30 seconds to create a great first impression and much of that message comes from the way you carry yourself (confident or unsure), posture (standing tall, head up, eyes forward, shoulders back), and facial expression (smiling, frowning). Clearly, even before we speak, our bodies telegraph our attitude and personality in great volume!

FIVE HAND HABITS THAT SEND THE WRONG MESSAGE

Hand and arm movement is important to conveying a message successfully. Here are my top five bad habits involving hand and arm gestures. They all interfere with positive and engaging kinesthetic messages.

1. **Hands Crossed in Front.** In his book *The Exceptional Presenter*, Timothy Koegel calls this position the "T-Rex" (think hands dangling from exceptionally short arms). It is a common mistake of presenters and speakers, who find this ingrained pattern of behavior hard to break. I consulted with a CEO who had a habit of using this position. Although he was a good

speaker who used his voice effectively to convey his message, this habit distracted from his presentation. He also folded his fingers, clasped his hands, played with his wedding ring, and sometimes appeared to be praying. Once he realized the impact that this had on his message, he eliminated the habit through practice.

2. **Hands in Pockets.** This bad habit communicates conflicting messages, none of them good, from being passive and non-confident to being cocky, overconfident, and defensive. Aside from those negative messages, hands in pockets prevent the speaker from using physical gestures that support the message and aid listeners in processing and storing the information being presented.

HOW HANDS CAN SUPPORT LEARNING

Hands support learning in many ways. Here are some examples of the power of even simple movement. Imagine how not using movement would undermine these simple statements.

1. Make or Enhance a Verbal Statement:
    - "Stop the activity" (hand up, palm out).
    - "Change partners" (swirling motion).
2. Prioritize Key Points:
    - "Point number 1 is. . . . Point number 2 is. . . .— (fingers showing the count as each number is verbalized).
3. Make Comparisons:
    - "The rise in applications from a low of 2,000 to today's high of 5,000 was driven mainly by. . . ." (movement of hands from a low position to a higher position).

---

3. **Hands Behind Back.** Speakers who keep their hands behind their backs project a message that they are unsure of themselves or the information they are communicating. Audiences might also assume that the speaker is not telling the truth or that some physical object is being hidden from them. No matter what the speaker's intentions, this habit derails audience trust and that believability gap directly impacts learning.

4. **Hands on Hips.** This is a classic power position that conveys control that you might use in front of the mirror before your presentation to build "superhero" confidence, but it's completely inappropriate on stage. Not only does this habit turn audiences off, but it discourages community and sharing in a training or learning environment and shuts down risk taking and experimentation among participants.

5. **Arms Crossed.** Crossed arms are another classic "closed" position that communicates a lack of responsiveness to conversation or opinion. The message is discomfort or disinterest or a statement that "you have the floor." A folded-arm position also communicates that you're not comfortable with your own body and that you are shutting off the audience from further conversation. Learning is a two-way street, and crossed arms indicates a one-way street.

WHAT TO DO WITH YOUR HANDS

So, where should your arms and hands be when you're not using them to help participants engage with the content you're presenting? The answer is simply resting at your side in a comfortable and natural position. Since most of us have developed a tendency to position our hands somewhere—in pockets, folded, crossed, holding anything available—when we're not using them, making this change will take some practice. You might work on this hand-resting position in social situations until it feels comfortable. However, for anyone who spends a lot of time in front of audiences, the payoff is that when you do use your hands in a presentation, the movements will have real expressive power that will help you make an emotional connection with your audience.

> *Emotional environment sets the stage for intellectual achievement.*
> Lee Oberparleiter, from his the graduate education course,
> "Brain-Based Teaching and Learning"

HOW TO BE A CONFIDENT KINESTHETIC PRESENTER AND TRAINER

Whether you're delivering a keynote address, conducting a workshop or a corporate training class, or presenting at a conference, your success is tied to how well you're able to connect emotionally with your audience. Excellent speaking technique—a strong, clear, well-modulated voice speaking in an inspirational tone—provides a base-line connection to your audience. Body language—good posture and confident attitude—is another level of connection, but without the kinesthetic element of movement, you won't achieve a visceral, emotional connection that supports change.

My preference for establishing an emotional connection with audiences is to tell a humorous, personal story. During the narration, I make eye contact with individual members of the audience to put everyone at ease. Once this connection is established, I am deliberate about how I use my body to maintain this connection during the presentation. At the same time, I carefully monitor audience "buy-in" of my presentation by asking myself the questions below.

Are audience members:

- Engaging by reflecting eye contact. Do they follow with their eyes as I move; does their body language say "interested"?
- Connected to the content and open to my message. Are they asking appropriate questions; do I see agreement in their body language (yes gesture with head) and verbal agreement.
- Participating in the moment by laughing when appropriate, clapping when appropriate, fully participating in activities, and taking notes.
- Committed to the action(s) I'm proposing? Is the verbal feedback in agreement; is the group communicating with me and the rest of the group in verbal and nonverbal ways.

The more confident and in-control you appear to your learners, the more effective you'll be at presenting and training. Here are some key ways you can make that apparent to audiences in both small and large venues.

1. **Good Posture Is Vital.**   Stand with shoulders back but relaxed. Just this simple, deliberate act will help you feel more in charge and confident.
2. **Be Generous with Friendly Eye Contact.**   If you maintain eye contact, you'll likely maintain your posture since this habit forces you head to stay up and connected.
3. **Smile Like You're Having Fun.**   If you appear to be having a good time, your posture is good and eye contact frequent, then you'll both disarm criticism and engage your audience.
4. **Move with Energy, Enthusiasm, and Purpose.**   Keep moving and active. It DOES engage your audience.

5. **Never Forget the Brain/Body Connection.**   Remember that your physiology directly impacts your psychology. If you're not feeling confident or engaged, use the other four techniques above—whether or not you're "feeling it"—and in most cases your energy and connect will return.

6. **Maximize Use of Your Physical Space.**   When making important points, use your physical space to reinforce it. This might mean closing the distance between you and the audience or a particular audience member. It might also mean using appropriate gestures to support your point rather than detract from it.

7. **Eliminate Nervous Mannerisms.**   I once worked with a client who had unusual hand mannerisms that were not present when he engaged in "normal" conversation. Because these mannerisms were uncomfortable to watch, his most important points were lost. His hands became the main show. Once he understood the impact of the mannerism and eliminated it, he became a much more powerful speaker. People have to be made aware of these very subconscious mannerisms. They can be pointed out and re-created, but anyone in presentation training should be videotaped. Correction of nervous mannerisms happens much more easily when the presenter can actually see the motion. It is then to be pointed out that only through constant and corrective practice is there a shot at eliminating the bad habit.

8. **Use Space Effectively.**   Simply pacing back and forth is not an effective use of space. This doesn't mean that the speaker should use more movement than is necessary, as too much movement can be irritating to your audience. Practice your talk or presentation to get an indication of where the important points are, what should be supported only by a gesture, a movement forward, a movement toward an individual who

serves as a proxy for the entire group, or the use of a grand gesture that includes the entire audience.

I have always choreographed my movements during presentations. Sometimes I stand up (sometimes on a chair), and other times I sit down (sometimes in the audience). I may stop my movement midstride to make an important point or accentuate my words with an announced movement. I plan and rehearse these movements so I know they'll work. Of course, these actions can be risky, so make sure they are properly linked to the content. A kinesthetic action that has nothing to do with what you're talking about could put a presentation in peril.

KEY CONCEPTS

■ The human brain is programmed to learn through movement. All presentations are kinesthetic presentations. It's just a matter of how much and how well. Body language communicates far more than words do.

■ Using the body effectively during a presentation creates an emotional bond with the audience and a heightened sense of interest. This helps with matters dealing with attention and retention.

■ Three important things to keep in mind when presenting are that movement engages the brain, physical gestures can be seen as inviting or distracting, and using movement and voice effectively creates an empathetic connection with the audience.

■ Be aware of your physical presentation habits that send the wrong the message.

KINESTHETIC PRESENTER PRINCIPLES WORKSHEET

This chapter discussed a variety of ways to ensure that you apply kinesthetic principles to become a more effective presenter. Think about each of the activities discussed and jot down how you are currently using or plan to use these principles in your future learning events.

Kinesthetic Principle	Currently Use	Plan to Use	How will you incorporate these presentation skills into current and future training programs?
Three Key Kinesthetic Presentation Techniques			
Use Movement to Engage the Brain Move about and within an audience rather than just back and forth the across the board room, podium, or stage.			
Use Inviting Physical Gestures Make sure your words and physical gestures are "in synch." The opposite can create a level of discomfort among your audience members.			
Connect Empathetically with the Audience Manage the "state" of your audience. Teaching from different parts of the room, modulating your voice, or providing a brain break manage the state of your audience, which is critical to the success of the training.			
Avoid Hand and Arm Movements That Send Wrong Message			
Hands Folded Allows for fidgeting.			
Hands in Pockets Suggests passivity or overconfidence			

(continues)

Kinesthetic Principle	Currently Use	Plan to Use	How will you incorporate these presentation skills into current and future training programs?
Hands Behind Back Says that you are unsure of yourself.			
Hands on Hips A power move that discourages community.			
Arms Folded A classic closed/uninterested gesture.			
Confident Trainer Characteristics			
Good Posture You send an immediate message with your body language and posture!			
Eye Contact Make sure your eyes are on the audience, shared generously with everyone and at times focused on one person in a way that still speaks to the entire audience.			
Have Fun Audiences love energy and having fun!			
Move with Energy Your body and movement says much more than your words!			
Use Brain/Body Connection We are brain/body speakers and audiences. Use this information to your advantage.			

Kinesthetic Principle	Currently Use	Plan to Use	How will you incorporate these presentation skills into current and future training programs?
Maximize Physical Space Use all the space that is available and appropriate.			
Avoid Nervous Mannerisms Your body should be as calm, cool, and collected as your voice.			
Effectively Use Space Important points are often made not by standing still but through the combination of effective voice, hand gestures, and body movements.			

Notes

1. http://www.psychologytoday.com/blog/beyond-words/201109/is-nonverbal
-communication-numbers-game.
2. http://www.forbes.com/sites/carolkinseygoman/2012/01/03/10-simple-and
-powerful-body-language-tips-for-2012/.
3. Oberparleiter, L. (2004). *Brain-based teaching and learning*. Department of Education, Gratz College. Graduate Course Trainers Manual. Randolph, NJ: Center for Lifelong Learning.

Why Movement Is a Powerful Learning Tool

A local high school recently asked me to speak to students at its annual career day. The invitation was a return engagement that came after the publication of my 2010 book, *The Kinesthetic Classroom: Teaching and Learning Through Movement*. As the first to speak that day, I was positioned onstage waiting for the students to file in and didn't initially notice the young woman standing on the floor at stage left motioning me over. But when she did catch my eye, I walked over and the young woman immediately stated her purpose.

"Weren't you here last year?" she said.

"Yes, I gave the keynote," I replied, a little flattered that she remembered.

"I thought so," she told me with some excitement. "I remember because you taught us how to learn SAT vocabulary words using our bodies and you taught us how to remember the meaning of words like obstinate."

"And why did you remember that word?" I asked.

She smiled, made a fist with her right hand, and began tapping it against her head. Then she said "hard-headed." Next, she used her hands to push away from her body and said "unyielding."

She laughed, told me she was looking forward to my talk, and then turned on her heels to scurry back to her waiting friends.

I recount this story because it provides a clear example of the most important underlying principle of this book—that movement enhances our brain's ability to learn and, more specifically as this story demonstrates, moves what we learn from temporary memory to permanent storage for later recall. More than a year had passed between the day my curious student had participated in the short demonstration activity I gave at my talk, yet she recalled exactly what she learned. For me, this is a perfect illustration of how the brain/body connection enhances the learning process.

TEACHING COMPLEX TOPICS

Movement is an effective tool for both simple and complex concepts. For example, if you were interested in having your learners remember the functional role of various chemicals in the brain, here's how you might structure the learning as a movement-based activity.

Neurons perform a vital connection role in our brain and ensure that various parts of the brain communicate with one another. Neurons have distinct parts that carry out specific functions—dendrites, nuclei and axons, a myelin sheath, and a release point for the neurotransmitters (it's not necessary to explain the function for this example). So to use movement in this example, you might tell learners that their fingers are dendrites, their palms are nuclei, their shirt sleeves are the myelin sheath (if someone is wearing a sleeveless shirt I would suggest they pretend to have a sleeve), and their elbows are the release point for the neurotransmitters.

Then, to graphically connect these brain chemical parts to their function all that's needed is a bit of creativity with the learners. You might hold up your fingers and wiggle them while asking what they represent—dendrites.

Then you might ask, "To what are the dendrites attached?", "the nucleus (and soma, or cell body)?" You would then follow these connections throughout the discussions and make this physical connection every time the key words are mentioned.

With this example, it's possible to include more memory bookmarks by making popping sounds that represent the neurons connecting electrically in the brain.

THE BODY IS AN EFFICIENT LEARNING TOOL

The body is a more efficient learning tool than we imagine because it's paired with a brain that prefers to learn by doing. Yet that does not mean it's possible or appropriate to always use this brain/body connection. As I've noted throughout this book, choosing the right tool is a judgment call. However, if movement-based learning activities are appropriate to teach critical content, then failure to do so means that a powerful learning tool has been left on the table. Here are some other advantages:

- Movement provides a welcome learning opportunity for kinesthetic learners (likely a majority of your training participants).
- Movement strengthens the ability to tap into our brain's preferred way to learn through implicit channels. As demonstrated in this book, attaching emotional value to learning enhances the experience, and kinesthetic activity creates positive emotional involvement with the content.

- Movement gives the brain an environmental (or episodic) advantage when trying to recall information by creating a "learning address" for content (where learning occurred).
- Movement provides additional sensory cues for the brain to store information. An additional pathway increases the chances more content will be stored and available for retrieval in the future.
- Movement increases motivation and focus. Using movement allows learners to stay focused on the moment. This engagement means learners enjoy the training and perceive that the training is moving along at a faster rate.

EDUCATION AND TRAINING

It's easy to incorporate movement in traditional education programs to teach anything from math to Shakespeare, but sometimes it takes a little creativity to bring movement into corporate training environments. However, here are some areas that the movement fit is a natural because within these areas of training there exists many opportunities to "learn by doing."

Learn by Doing

When I teach presentation skills, I purposely spend the bulk of the class time allowing participants to learn by doing. Sure, I could spend a day describing the core competencies of an effective speaker, but that's not nearly as an effective approach as giving learners an actual opportunity to speak and experience learning critique and correct practice. The bottom line is that you learn to speak by speaking and to present effectively through actually presenting. You do not learn by simply discussing the best techniques. Pilots are trained in simulators that can create any situation they might encounter in a plane. This type of learning, often taken for granted in a stand-and-deliver type of training, is as essential to the success of any trainee as it is to a pilot. Consider the following training scenarios:

- **Time and Productivity Management.** Participants are allowed to specifically use and practice time management skills in a real context.
- **Customer Service.** Trainees role-play phone and face-to-face customer-service skills so they are second nature when faced with any customer-service situation.
- **Effective Meeting Management.** Trainees are given meeting topics so they can design the entire process and run a mock meeting.
- **Correct Hiring Practices.** Trainees are allowed to experience all aspects of correct hiring practices, especially the interviewing process, which is an art in itself.
- **Managing Constant Change.** Trainees are given scenarios that require leadership through change and lead teams through the process.
- **Stress Management.** Trainees are taken through specific stress managements techniques, such as autogenic training, mindfulness practice, meditation, and progressive muscle relaxation.
- **Technical Training.** This may be the most obvious but learning the latest technology can be best achieved by diving in and practicing the technology itself. This is based on the user's technical knowledge and how he or she can compare a new technology to something already known. For those who would be unfamiliar with technology, someone has to actually guide them in a sensible way.

Consider this a starter list only. I am sure with just a little thought you could expand this list. In general, any topic or skill development learning program with any "doing" or "experiential" aspect has potential for movement-based activities. Even topics such as legal compliance, financial management, or basic accounting can take advantage of this brain/body connection. Here is example from a corporate wellness training program I conducted recently at a manufacturing plant in southeastern Pennsylvania.

Using Movement in Creative Ways

Clearly, wellness is a topic that lends itself to using movement activities. However, I didn't have a lot of time for my segment of the program, and the participants were coming to my session after sitting through other classes. As a result, I knew I would have an attention issue, which meant I had the perfect opportunity to introduce a brain break.

When the learners were assembled in my class, I decided to begin with some general overview statistics about wellness in America. I wanted the participants to know that according to the Center for Disease Control (CDC), 1 in 3 children born in the year 2000 will develop diabetes and that this ratio is 1 in 2 for African American or Latino people. It's a sobering statistic that could have been presented nicely with a pie chart in a PowerPoint slide, but instead I made this statistic real by allowing the audience to be part of the learning.

I noted that it's hard to really understand the real world impact of statistics, so I told participants that this activity would help them make the connection. The room happened to be arranged in nine neat rows of chairs. First, I asked all the participants to stand next to the chairs; then, I gave them the diabetes statistics. I asked them to imagine that everyone in the room was born in the year 2000. Then, I issued the following directions:

- Everyone in the first three rows, please sit down.
- Now, everyone sitting in the next three rows please sit down.

- According to the diabetes statistic I gave you, everyone in these first six rows will not develop diabetes.
- Everyone in the last three rows and still standing is likely to develop diabetes.

I reminded the participants that this 1 in 3 statistic was the general population statistic for children born in 2000. Then I asked everyone to stand up again and reminded the participants that the statistic was 1 in 2 for African Americans and Latinos.

- With everyone standing again, I asked 50 percent of the audience to sit down. I pointed out that all those standing would, according to this CDC statistic, develop diabetes in their lifetimes.

This impromptu activity was successful because it:

- Used the body as a learning tool by making the information much more memorable and useable.
- Provided a brain break.
- Made an emotional connection to the content.
- Created a physical, meaningful interaction with the presenter and offered a comprehensible visual to a statistic.

Reviewing and teaching content using movement, or kinesthetic activity, can seem like a daunting task but it's worth the effort. Movement is a natural experience for the brain and one in which most learners will thrive if given the proper exposure in the right amount of doses.

OTHER BENEFITS OF MOVEMENT:
CORPORATE WELLNESS

In Chapter 4, it was mentioned earlier that recent research published in the *Journal of the National Cancer Institute* indicated that an extra two hours of sitting per day increased your risk of colon, endometrial, and lung cancers.[1] The research did not prove cause and effect, but it did show a link between sedentary behaviors and an increased risk for certain cancers. Other research has shown that even regular exercise can't counterbalance the ill effects of hours of sitting. We are built to move; our bodies beg to be used. Nilofer Merchant, author and business leader, eloquently stated it this way in her TED (Technology, Entertainment, and Design) talk, "Sitting has become the smoking of our generation."[2]

Another interesting piece of research came out of Washington University in St. Louis. The behavioral researchers wanted to explore group dynamics in meetings without chairs. Teams worked on creating a university recruitment video in rooms that either had chairs arranged around a table or had no chairs at all. The university's press release stated quite clearly, "University participants in the study who stood had greater physiological arousal and were less territorial about ideas than those in the seated arrangement. Members of the standing groups reported that their team members were less protective of their ideas. This reduced territoriality, led to more information sharing and to higher-quality university recruitment videos."[3]

The power of recognizing the brain and body as one in all aspects of life, whether it be training or physical and mental health, cannot be overstated. It is all connected. Researchers will be trying to connect all the dots for the good part of this century.

The research that underlies this book does demonstrate that aerobic exercise produces better cognitive results. For the purpose of this book, that means better results for learners.

How can I connect fitness to training? Easily. First, researchers now know without hesitation that aerobic exercise produces better cognitive results and that one of the primary beneficiaries of the benefits of aerobic activity is the brain, which means better trainees. Secondly, what is good for the heart is good for the brain, which means healthy trainees. Third, wellness is the pinnacle of the brain/body connection, which is a critical piece of training. In the larger view, here are some of the benefits to having physically fit employees:

- Motivation
- Better Health
- Less Stress
- Greater Cognitive Function
- Greater Levels of Presenteeism
- Lower Levels of Absenteeism
- More Productive Employees

Edward Stanley, the Third Earl of Derby, says it this way, "Those who think they have not time for bodily exercise will sooner or later have to find time for illness." Far too many people test his theory. All you aspire to be is jeopardized by an inactive lifestyle. Exercise provides a better brain, body, and perspective, which make you more effective. It is simplistic at its core, yet remains elusive for many.

Aerobic exercise, such as walking, jogging, swimming, and cycling, lowers blood sugar, insulin levels, and blood pressure. It also reduces stress and raises good cholesterol. Physically active people enjoy better bone, lung, and heart health, and have an easier time managing their weight. But these are all side effects. The true beneficiary of aerobic fitness is your brain.

Over the last several decades researchers have discovered some exciting characteristics about the relationship between exercise and the brain. According to Ratey, a lack of aerobic exercise impairs cognitive function especially as we age. He says, "Exercise is like Miracle-Gro for the brain."[3]

Ratey taught me that aerobic exercise is nature's natural antidote to serious ailments, such as depression, addiction, ADHD, and Alzheimer's disease. We are designed to move. It is a part of our natural make-up. Sedentary lifestyles are not natural to the human existence. In fact, they run contrary to our genetic design.

All of us experience periodic stress. Thankfully, our bodies are well equipped for the challenge. Unfortunately, chronic stress has become a characteristic of modern life and that is problematic, both personally and professionally. The good news is that any aerobic activity is an effective stress manager. How could it not be? Swimming, running, cycling, or hiking all demand our focus and attention. Exercise epitomizes living in the moment, where stressful thoughts are not allowed. On a biological level, exercise puts your body in a stressful situation, and in short doses, it is not only healthful, but necessary. I look forward to my workouts, in part because I know I will experience active stress relief. You could equate exercising with receiving a low dose vaccination—to combat stress. Exercising in response to stress is a simple and effective way to raise your body's ability to deal with the pressures of everyday life. As with meditation or deep breathing, exercise calms the body, making it possible to manage greater levels of turbulence.

Try this simple experiment. The next time you feel overwhelmed by stress, hit the road, jump in the pool, get on your bike, or go for a walk and don't stop for 30 minutes. When you've finished your workout, notice what has happened to your stress levels. They will have lessened, if not completely vanished. It is real, it is biological, and it can always be counted on.

Notes

1. Schmid, D. & Leitzmann, M. (2014). Television viewing and time spent sedentary in relation to cancer risk: A meta-analysis. *Journal of the National Cancer Institute,* 106(7): dju098 doi:10.1093/jnci/dju098.
2. Merchant, N. (2013). *Got a meeting? Take a walk.* Monterey, CA: TED.
3. Knight, A.P., & Baer, M. Get up, stand up: The effects of a non-sedentary workspace on information elaboration and group performance. *Social Psychological and Personality Science, 5(8),* 910–917.
4. Ratey, J. (2008). *SPARK: The Revolutionary New Science of Exercise and the Brain.* New York: Little, Brown and Company.

Appendixes

- Appendix 1—Glossary
- Appendix 2—Worksheets and Handouts
- Appendix 3—Other Resources

Glossary

Term	Definition
Aerobic Exercise	Physical exercise of a lower intensity that uses oxygen to adequately meet energy demands.
Amygdala	Structure located in the limbic system in the center of the brain that processes emotion and encodes emotional messages to long-term memory.
Automatic Memory	Located in the cerebellum and is reflexive by nature.
Axon	Part of a neuron that is a long fiber that relays messages from the cell to the receiving neuron.
Brain Break	Use of physical activity to provide a break from content in order to refocus, reenergize, and create more efficient learners.
Brain Stem	A part of the brain that monitors basic body functions, such as digestion, heart rate, body temperature, and respiration.

Term	Definition
Cerebellum	Part of the brain that coordinates movement and the performance and timing of complex motor tasks.
Cerebrum	The largest part of the brain by size and weight. Plays an important role in thinking, memory, speech, and movement.
Chunking	Breaking large amounts of content into smaller, more readily learnable bits of material, thereby making it possible for the brain to perceive the larger amount as one chunk.
Corpus Callosum	Thick bundle of nerve fibers that connects the two hemispheres of the brain.
Cross-Lateral	Movements that intentionally cross the midline of the body.
Dendrite	Part of a neuron that receives impulses from neighboring neurons. Dendrites are branches that extend from the cell body.
Differentiation	A popular teaching technique in K–12 education that focuses on recognizing learner's differences related to readiness, interest, or learning profile. This technique can be extended to most training scenarios.
Dopamine	Neurotransmitter associated with movement, pleasure, mood, sleep, and working memory.
Emotional Memory	The most powerful of all memory lanes; the retention of the emotional attributes of an experience.
Engagement	Level of attention during a training or learning experience.
Episodic Memory	Environmental or location memory processed by the hippocampus.

Term	Definition
Explicit Learning	Labeled type of learning of a semantic nature that normally includes things like discussion, reading, listening, lectures, worksheets, and the like.
Frontal Lobe	Located in the front of the brain, it regulates emotional excess, processes higher order thinking, and allows for problem solving, planning, and thinking.
Hippocampus	A limbic system structure that encodes information from working memory to long-term memory and also compares new information with that already stored.
Implicit Learning	Acquisition of knowledge that normally takes place beyond our conscious awareness.
Kinesthetic	Refers to using movement in different contexts in teaching, training, and learning.
Long-Term Memory and Storage	The process of how (memory) and the area in (storage) the cerebrum where memories are permanently stored.
Melatonin	Neurotransmitter associated with sleep/wake cycle.
Motivation	Reasons for acting in a particular way; the influence of the meeting of needs on behavior.
Myelin	A fatty substance that surrounds, protects, and insulates the axon of a neuron.
Nucleus	The central part of a neuron.
Neurogenesis	The process of growing new nerve cells.
Neuron	A type of brain cell that sends and receives information through electrical and chemical signals.
Neurotransmitter	One of several dozen chemicals that transmit impulses from one neuron to another.

Term	Definition
Novelty	A training technique that provides for new, different, or interesting events to create a state change.
Partnering	A way to have individual learners pair with each other to complete a given assignment.
Practice	The repetition of a skill.
Primacy-Recency Effect	The phenomenon whereby one tends to remember best that which comes first in a learning episode and second best that which comes last (Sousa, 2011).
Procedural Memory	Allows for the learning and recall of motor and cognitive skills.
Rehearsal	The reprocessing of information in working memory.
Retention	Information stored for the long term that can be retrieved and recalled accurately.
Semantic Memory	Having to do with words, facts, and data unrelated to an event.
Short-Term Memory	Memory with a defined span and not stored for the long term.
State Management	Self- or trainer-directed management of a learner's brain/body emotional state.
Synapse	The gap between the axon of one neuron and the dendrite of another.
Working Memory	A temporary memory where processing of information occurs on a conscious level.

Worksheets and Handouts

CHAPTER 2

EIGHT BRAIN PRINCIPLES WORKSHEET

This chapter discussed eight key ways that our brains prefer to receive, process, and store information. Review each of the preferences cited and jot down how you currently use or plan to use these principles in your learning events.

Learning Preference	Currently Use	Plan to Use	How will you incorporate these learning preferences into current and future training programs?
Our brain is preprogramed to notice novelty in the surrounding environment. Changing up the environment resets this innate scanning switch and allows for focused attention from your learners.			

(*continues*)

Learning Preference	Currently Use	Plan to Use	How will you incorporate these learning preferences into current and future training programs?
Learning and movement are innately connected in the human brain. That's why learning new concepts and taking in new information through the use of our bodies is one of the most effective learning technologies available to trainers. It's all about implicit learning—the brain's preferred way to learn.			
Learning is enhanced when we connect and communicate with others. Managing this basic need for connection and community in your classroom will increase the likelihood that more of the information you present will be stored in long-term memory and retained for later use.			
Emotional connection enhances the learning experience. If a strong enough emotion is detected, the amygdala may encode the memory with an emotional tag.			
Learn by doing is a fundamental learning preference. The most effective training is hands-on, concrete, and directly applicable to what actions are required to produce the desirable outcome.			

Learning Preference	Currently Use	Plan to Use	How will you incorporate these learning preferences into current and future training programs?
Connecting new knowledge to old knowledge improves retention. Our brains are wired to make this connection, and we feel good when we connect the new information with the old.			
Down time is required to ensure new learning is processed and stored. Short bursts of content should be followed by review, practice, and rehearsal activity to provide the opportunity for information to be transferred to the permanent memory lock box and is supported by repetition and time away from learning activities. A retention check (in a multiday learning event) should be done the next day to make sure sleep has done its job to firmly cement the content in long-term memory.			
Down time is required to ensure new learning is processed and stored. A low-stress, highly engaging environment works best to encourage learning.			

CHAPTER 3

BENEFITS OF MOVEMENT WORKSHEET

The magic of movement is very real because it changes the brain in ways that enhance the learning process in eight specific ways. Based on your reading of this chapter, makes some notes about how you might incorporate movement benefits into your own training programs. As you work through the book, pay particular attention to additional information, tips, or techniques that will help meet these needs and jot down some notes on why this benefit is currently so important.

Benefit of Movement	How will you incorporate these movement principles into current and future training programs?
Allows for Implicit Learning Implicit learning takes place beyond our conscious awareness. Training often relies on explicit channels, such as PowerPoint slides, discussion, exercises, and memorization, but these methods don't align with the brain's preferred pathways. It's the difference between learning how to do something like replace a light bulb by watching it done and then doing it yourself and reading a precise and detailed description about how to do it.	
Provides a Break and Refocuses Attention Working memory (akin to a computer's RAM) has limited capacity for retention. Training often overloads our brain's RAM without allowing time for processing and storing information. That's why shorter bits of information are better. Movement refocuses participant attention to allow time for the brain to store new information and prepare it to receive new content.	
Creates Motivation Movement promotes five key human needs that underpin human motivation: survival, belonging, power, freedom, and fun. Training participants who have these needs met are more motivated learners.	

Benefit of Movement	How will you incorporate these movement principles into current and future training programs?
Improves the Learning State Participants develop a positive learning state, in which a balance exists between a participant's emotional state (interest and focus on the topic) and physical state (hungry and uncomfortable). Trainers should be keenly aware when these states are out of balance.	
Differentiates Training The most effective trainers do their best to accommodate the different learning styles favored by participants, but such accommodation is not always possible. That's why the introduction is so important. It offers a well-documented avenue for learning.	
Engages the Senses Our brains crave sensory cues, such as listening, writing, watching, hearing, and discussing, to facilitate the learning process. Movement adds another layer to the learning senses and in particular adds strength to the powerful senses that contribute most to learning—seeing, hearing, and touching.	
Reduces Stress Movement produces dopamine in our brains, often called the feel-good hormone. The production of this hormone reduces stress, and less stress means more learning potential for participants.	
Enhances Episodic Learning and Memory Information is easier to recall when it's paired with a dynamic experience, so that concepts linked to movement make them easier to recall when needed.	

CHAPTER 4

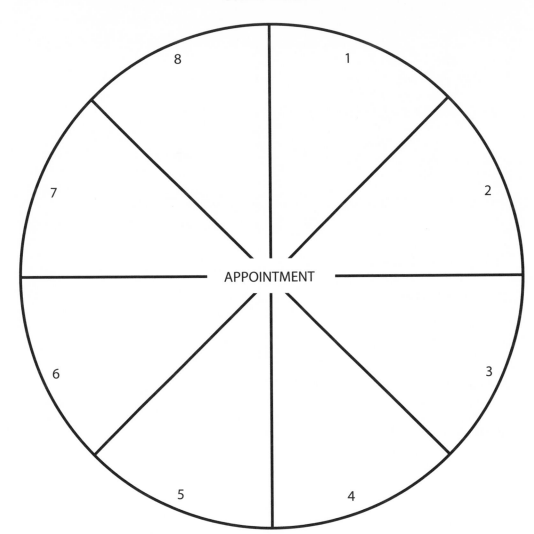

SAMPLE QUOTE PARTNERS WORKSHEET

If you can dream it, you can do it.

Walt Disney, business magnate and animator

Partner #1 _____

Setting goals is the first step in turning the invisible into the visible.

Tony Robbins, life coach and self-help author

Partner #2 _____

You can never quit. Winners never quit, and quitters never win.

Ted Turner, media mogul and philanthropist

Partner #3 _____

If you've got a talent, protect it.

Jim Carrey, actor and comedian

Partner #4 _____

I'm intimidated by the fear of being average.

Taylor Swift, singer and songwriter

Partner #5 _____

18 BRAIN-BREAKS WORKSHEET

This chapter discussed 18 activities to encourage brain breaks. Review each of the activities discussed and jot down how you are currently using or planning to use these principles in your future learning events.

Brain-Break Activities	Currently Use	Plan to Use	How will you incorporate these brain-break activities into current and future training programs?
Time for a Partner Participants partner with each other using an 8-, 10-, or 12-segment "clock" that encourages connection with other participants.			
Famous Quotes This is an alternative activity to Clock Partners that uses quotes as a way to partner versus time for a partner.			
Walk 'n' Talk Participants partner and go for a walk together to provide time and movement to discuss training-related content.			
1-2-3 Math! A variation on rock, paper, scissors to solve simple math equations.			
Finger Snatch Partners try to grab the finger of their partner while simultaneously trying to prevent their partner from grabbing their own finger.			
Handshake Fact Participants review material each time they find one of five different partners with whom to shake hands.			

Brain-Break Activities	Currently Use	Plan to Use	How will you incorporate these brain-break activities into current and future training programs?
Back-to-Back Low Five While standing back to back, partners swing to the same side at the same time and give each other low fives as quickly as possible.			
Nose/Ear Switch While grabbing their noses and crossing over to the opposite ear with the other hand, participants are asked to switch hand positions.			
Stand Up When You Know Instead of the standard practice of raising one's hand to answer a question, participants are asked to stand up when they know an answer.			
Content Switch Whenever there is a significant change in material or content, participants are asked to change seats. Good for episodic or environmental memory.			
Simple Exercise This is a simple exercise break through the use of any number of activities, including walking in place, stretching, and doing cross-laterals, light yoga and the like.			
Discussion Movement When learning dictates group discussion, this activity moves participants to specific areas in the room where they stand and discuss.			

(*continues*)

Brain-Break Activities	Currently Use	Plan to Use	How will you incorporate these brain-break activities into current and future training programs?
Improvisational Throw Participants circle up and toss imaginary objects to one another, throwing and receiving as if they are real.			
Silent Introductions Participants are asked to introduce themselves to each other through descriptive movements only—no talking.			
Vacation Writing Participants use different parts of their bodies to "air" write the answers to specific questions about their favorite vacations.			
Please Stand Up This is an alternative to simply asking your learners to stand up and stretch for their brain break.			
Stand and Breathe Full deep breathing is the first doorway to relaxation—and in our case to a brain break.			
Stand and Squeeze A surprisingly effective brain break that combines the relaxation benefits of breathing and a technique for progressive muscle relaxation.			

CHAPTER 5

GOAL-SETTING WORKSHEET

Use this Ankle Walk debrief sheet to help your team improve their performance and meet their goals during the activity.

Step 1—PLAN Your Vision. Team members must walk 10 to 15 feet as a single unit without their touching feet losing contact. What is your vision for achieving this goal?

- ◼ _____
- ◼ _____
- ◼ _____
- ◼ _____

Step 2—LIST Your Actions. What strategies will you use to accomplish this goal?

- ◼ _____
- ◼ _____
- ◼ _____
- ◼ _____

Step 3—ASSESS the Outcomes. How well did the plan work?

- ◼ _____
- ◼ _____
- ◼ _____
- ◼ _____

Step 4—NEW Approach (if necessary). If the original plan fails, what new strategy would you develop and execute?

- ◼ _____
- ◼ _____
- ◼ _____
- ◼ _____

10 TEAM-BUILDING ACTIVITIES WORKSHEET

This chapter discussed 10 activities designed to encourage the building of relationships and community among team members. Review each of the activities discussed and jot down how you are currently using or plan to use these principles in your future learning events.

Team-Building Activities	Currently Use	Plan to Use	How will you incorporate these team-building activities into current and future training programs?
Ankle Walk This activity helps participants meet and achieve goals by encouraging follow through.			
Floating Balloon A fun team-building activity that encourages movement, laughter, and working to support one another.			
Learn My Name Allows for learning new names in a fun and fast-paced setting.			
I Wish I Could Allows participants to learn new and interesting facts about each other.			
Name Tag Switch Helps build a collegial community by discovering the identity of someone through the writing and sharing of a simple sentence.			
Shared Unique Experiences A set of unusual questions are answered in a movement-oriented setting that creates bonds among different team members.			

Team-Building Activities	Currently Use	Plan to Use	How will you incorporate these team-building activities into current and future training programs?
Rock, Paper, Scissors, Tag A fast-paced version of an oldie but goody that will have your participants' heart rates up and changing teams on a moment-to-moment basis.			
Elbow to Elbow A circle pass game using only a ball or balloon held between participants' elbows as the passing mechanism.			
Triangle Tag A fast-paced activity that builds team protection for one participant and creates the metaphor for how important teammates can be.			
The Human Touch A simple activity that shows how important the support of a teammate can be.			

CHAPTER 6

1	2	3	4	5
6	7	8	9	10
11	12	13	14	15
16	17	18	19	20

Figure 6.1 Trade Review Handout

CONTENT-REVIEW ACTIVITIES WORKSHEET

This chapter discussed five activities designed to enable successful content review. Think about each of the activities discussed and jot down how you are currently using or plan to use these principles in your future learning events.

Content-Review Activities	Currently Use	Plan to Use	How will you incorporate these content-review activities into current and future training programs?
Take and Talk The winner of the "grab" must answer a content-review question in this activity. If the correct answer is given, the winning player receives points for the round.			
Review at "The Improv" Group members review concepts in a role-play setting by acting out of concepts.			
Group Webbing on the Move Team members comment and question content listed in a web format on poster paper. They then move on to all assigned posters around the room to continue to comment and question each other's work.			
The "Moving" Venn Diagram Review Groups are given content cards and instructed to place them in the appropriate sides of a Venn diagram created with hula-hoops.			
The Trade Review Participants are asked to answer questions and then move to the center of the group circle to trade questions with another group member.			

CHAPTER 7

KINESTHETIC PRESENTER PRINCIPLES WORKSHEET

This chapter discussed a variety of ways to ensure that you apply kinesthetic principles to become a more effective presenter. Think about each of the activities discussed and jot down how you are currently using or plan to use these principles in your future learning events.

Kinesthetic Principle	Currently Use	Plan to Use	How will you incorporate these presentation skills into current and future training programs?
Three Key Kinesthetic Presentation Techniques			
Use Movement to Engage the Brain Move about and within an audience rather than just back and forth the across the board room, podium, or stage.			
Use Inviting Physical Gestures Make sure your words and physical gestures are "in synch." The opposite can create a level of discomfort among your audience members.			
Connect Empathetically with the Audience Manage the "state" of your audience. Teaching from different parts of the room, modulating your voice, or providing a brain break manage the state of your audience, which is critical to the success of the training.			
Avoid Hand and Arm Movements That Send Wrong Message			
Hands Folded Allows for fidgeting.			
Hands in Pockets Suggests passivity or overconfidence			

Kinesthetic Principle	Currently Use	Plan to Use	How will you incorporate these presentation skills into current and future training programs?
Hands Behind Back Says that you are unsure of yourself.			
Hands on Hips A power move that discourages community.			
Arms Folded A classic closed/uninterested gesture.			
Confident Trainer Characteristics			
Good Posture You send an immediate message with your body language and posture!			
Eye Contact Make sure your eyes are on the audience, shared generously with everyone and at times focused on one person in a way that still speaks to the entire audience.			
Have Fun Audiences love energy and having fun!			
Move with Energy Your body and movement says much more than your words!			
Use Brain/Body Connection We are brain/body speakers and audiences. Use this information to your advantage.			

Kinesthetic Principle	Currently Use	Plan to Use	How will you incorporate these presentation skills into current and future training programs?
Maximize Physical Space Use all the space that is available and appropriate.			
Avoid Nervous Mannerisms Your body should be as calm, cool, and collected as your voice.			
Effectively Use Space Important points are often made not by standing still but through the combination of effective voice, hand gestures, and body movements.			

Other Resources

BOOKS

Silberman, M. (2006). *Active Training*. Hoboken, NJ: Pfeiffer.

Jensen, E. (2000). *Learning with the body in mind*. Thousand Oaks: Corwin.

Jensen, E. (2005). *Teaching with the brain in mind*. Alexandria, VA: Association for Supervision and Curriculum Development.

Lengel, T. & Kuczala, M. (2010). *The Kinesthetic Classroom: Teaching and Learning through Movement*. Thousand Oaks: Corwin.

Ratey, J. (2008). Spark: *The revolutionary new science of exercise and the brain*. New York: Little, Brown.

Rosen, L.D. (2010). *Rewired: Understanding the iGeneration and the way they learn*. New York: Palgrave Macmillan.

Sladkey, D. (2013). *Energizing brain breaks*. Thousand Oaks: Corwin.

Sousa, D. (2011). *How the Brain Learns*. Thousand Oaks: Corwin.

Stolovitch, H. & Keeps, E. (2011). *Telling ain't training*. Alexandria, VA: American Society for Training and Development.

INTERNET SITES

Note: All sites were active at time of publication.

David L. Katz, MD, MPH, FACPM, FACP <http://www.davidkatzmd.com>.
Dr. Katz is the founding director of Yale University's Prevention Research Center and the Editor-in-Chief of the journal *Childhood Obesity*. Among many other resources at this site, Dr. Katz has created something called ABEs or Activity Bursts for Everyone <abeforfitness.com>.

Action Based Learning <http://www.abllab.com>/.
This is the website of Jean Blaydes Moize, a thought leader in the field of movement and learning. Here you will find products, services, and scholarly research related to movement and learning.

Learning and the Brain Conferences/Seminars <http://www.learningandthebrain.com>.
Learning & the Brain provides educational Conferences, Symposiums and Summer Institutes and one-day professional development training seminars on the latest research in neuroscience and psychology and their potential applications to education.

American Society for Training and Development now Association for Talent Development <http://www.astd.org>.
ASTD/ATD provides a comprehensive menu of resources for the trainer including publications, seminars, online training, face-to-face training, certifications, and conferences.

International Mind, Brain, and Education Society <http://www.imbes.org>.
IMBES facilitates cross-cultural collaboration in biology, education, and the cognitive and developmental sciences to improve knowledge, create and develop resources, and create research directions and educational practice.

Index

About the Author

Mike Kuczala is the coauthor the Corwin Bestseller and Association of Educational Publishers' Distinguished Achievement Award nominated, *The Kinesthetic Classroom: Teaching and Learning Through Movement,* a book and philosophy that has changed the view of teaching and learning around the world. Founder and President of Kuczala Consulting Inc. and Director of Instruction for the Regional Training Center, an educational consulting firm based in Randolph, New Jersey, Mike has become an in-demand keynote speaker and consultant at international conferences, school districts, and corporations. His standing room only presentations have been experienced in such diverse settings as The Forum for Innovative Leadership, the Association for Supervision and Curriculum Development, the American Association for Health, Physical Education, Recreation and Dance, and the Lawyer Brain Roundtable.

An expert in training, training design, and effective presentation, Mike has designed or codesigned three of the most successful graduate courses in the history of the Regional Training Center: *Motivation: The Art and Science of Inspiring Classroom Success, Wellness:*

Creating Health and Balance in the Classroom, and *The Kinesthetic Classroom: Teaching and Learning through Movement.* They are facilitated by a cadre of more than 70 trained instructors who have taught thousands of teachers the key principles of instructional movement, motivation, and wellness. Mike now works with corporations to enhance their sales training, presentation skill, corporate wellness, and effective training design and implementation.

As a graduate instructor, keynote speaker, and workshop presenter, Mike regularly facilitates professional development programs in both corporate and educational settings in the areas of motivation, presentation skill, using movement to enhance the learning process, brain-based teaching and training, differentiated instruction and training, enhancing student thinking, and topics related to wellness and stress management. His engaging and practical professional development programs have been enjoyed by tens of thousands of corporate executives, teachers, administrators, and parents across the United States over the last decade.

Connect with Mike Kuczala:
Website: www.mikekuczala.com
Twitter: @kinestheticlass